EX LIBRIS · EX LIBRIS · EX LIBRIS · EX LIBRIS · EX LIBRIS · EX LIBRIS · EX LIBRIS · EX LIBRIS · EX LIBRIS · EX

Rosie Friday

ABSURD
PERSON
SINGULAR

ABSURD
PERSON
SINGULAR

by Alan Ayckbourn

NELSON DOUBLEDAY, Inc.
Garden City, New York

ABSURD PERSON SINGULAR opened at the Music Box Theatre in New York City on October 8, 1974. It was presented by the Theatre Guild and the John F. Kennedy Center for the Performing Arts in association with Michael Codron. The director was Eric Thompson; scenery was designed by Edward Burbridge; costumes were designed by Levino Verna for Laurence Gross; and lighting was by Thomas Skelton. The cast, in order of appearance, was as follows:

Jane	Carole Shelley
Sidney	Larry Blyden
Ronald	Richard Kiley
Marion	Geraldine Page
Eva	Sandy Dennis
Geoffrey	Tony Roberts

ABSURD PERSON SINGULAR was first produced at the Library Theatre, Scarborough, in June 1972 and subsequently by Michael Codron at the Criterion Theatre, London, opening on July 4, 1973. The director was Eric Thompson and the settings were designed by Alan Tagg. The cast, in order of appearance, was as follows:

Jane	Bridget Turner
Sidney	Richard Briers
Ronald	Michael Aldridge
Marion	Sheila Hancock
Eva	Anna Calder-Marshall
Geoffrey	David Burke

ABSURD PERSON SINGULAR

A town in England. Time—the present.

ABSURD
PERSON
SINGULAR

ACT ONE

Sidney and Jane Hopcroft's kitchen of their small suburban house. Last Christmas.

Although on a modest scale, it is a model kitchen. While not containing all the gadgetry, it does have an automatic washing-machine, a fridge, an electric stove and a gleaming sink unit. All these are contained or surrounded by smart formica-topped working surfaces with the usual drawers and cupboards. The room also contains a small table, also formica-topped, and matching chairs.

When the curtain rises, Jane, a woman in her thirties, is bustling round wiping the floor, cupboard doors, working surfaces —in fact, anything in sight—with a cloth. She sings happily as she works. She wears a pinafore and bedroom slippers, but, under this, a smart new party dress. She is unimaginatively made up and her hair is tightly permed. She wears rubber gloves to protect her hands.

As Jane works, Sidney enters, a small dapper man of about the same age. He has a small trimmed moustache and a cheery, unflappable manner. He wears his best, rather old-fashioned, sober suit. A dark tie, polished hair and shoes complete the picture.

Sidney: Hallo, hallo. What are we up to out here, eh?
Jane: (*without pausing in her work*) Just giving it a wipe.
Sidney: Dear oh dear. Good gracious me. Does it need it? Like a battleship. Just like a battleship. They need you in the Royal Navy.

Jane: (*giggling*) Silly . . .
Sidney: No—the Royal Navy.
Jane: Silly . . .

Sidney goes to the back door, turns the Yale knob, opens it and sticks his hand out.

Sidney: Still raining, I see.
Jane: Shut the door, it's coming in.
Sidney: Cats and dogs. Dogs and cats. (*He shuts the door, wiping his wet hand on his handkerchief. Striding to the centre of the room and staring up at his digital clock*) Eighteen-twenty-three. (*Consulting his watch*) Eighteen-twenty-three. Getting on. Seven minutes—they'll be here.
Jane: Oh. (*She straightens up and looks around the kitchen for somewhere she's missed*)
Sidney: I've got a few games lined up.
Jane: Games?
Sidney: Just in case.
Jane: Oh good.
Sidney: I've made a parcel for "Pass the Parcel," sorted out a bit of music for musical bumps and thought out a few forfeits.
Jane: Good.
Sidney: I've thought up some real devils. (*He puts his leg on the table*)
Jane: I bet. (*She knocks his leg off, and wipes*)
Sidney: Just in case. Just in case things need jollying up. (*Seeing Jane still wiping*) I don't want to disappoint you but we're not going to be out here for our drinks, you know.
Jane: Yes, I know.
Sidney: The way you're going . . .
Jane: They might want to look . . .
Sidney: I doubt it.
Jane: The ladies might.

4

Sidney: (*chuckling knowingly*) I don't imagine the wife of a banker will particularly choose to spend her evening in our kitchen. Smart as it is.

Jane: No?

Sidney: I doubt if she spends very much time in her own kitchen. Let alone ours.

Jane: Still . . .

Sidney: Very much the lady of leisure, Mrs. Brewster-Wright. Or so I would imagine.

Jane: What about Mrs. Jackson?

Sidney: (*doubtfully*) Well—again, not a woman you think of in the same breath as you would a kitchen.

Jane: All women are interested in kitchens. (*She turns to the sink*)

Sidney: (*ironically*) Oh, if you're looking for a little job . . .

Jane: What's that?

Sidney: A small spillage. My fault.

Jane: (*very alarmed*) Where?

Sidney: In there. On the sideboard.

Jane: Oh, Sidney. (*She snatches up an assortment of cloths, wet and dry*)

Sidney: Nothing serious.

Jane: Honestly.

Sidney goes to the back door, opens it, sticks a hand out.

Sidney: Dear oh dear. (*He closes the door and dries his hand on his handkerchief*)

Jane: (*returning*) Honestly.

Sidney: Could you see it?

Jane: You spoil that surface if you leave it. You leave a ring. (*She returns her dish cloth to the sink, her dry cloths to the drawer and now takes out a duster and a tin of polish*) Now that room's going to smell of polish. I had the windows open all day so it wouldn't.

Sidney: Well then, don't polish.

5

Jane: I have to polish. There's a mark. (*She goes to the door and then pauses*) I know, bring the air freshener.

Sidney: Air freshener?

Jane: Under the sink. (*She goes out*)

Sidney: Ay, ay, Admiral. (*He whistles a sailor's horn-pipe, amused*) Dear oh dear. (*He opens the cupboard under the sink, rummages and brings out an aerosol tin. He is one of those men who likes to read all small print. This he does, holding the tin at arm's length to do so. Reading*) "Shake can before use." (*He does so. Reading*) "Remove cap." (*He does so. Reading*) "Hold away from body and spray into air by depressing button." (*He holds the can away from his body, points it in the air and depresses the button. The spray hisses out over his shirt front*) Dear oh dear. (*He puts down the tin, wipes his shirt-front with a dishcloth*)

Jane: (*entering*) What are you doing?

Sidney: Just getting this to rights. Just coming to terms with your air freshener.

Jane: That's the fly spray.

Sidney: Ah.

Jane: Honestly. (*She takes the canister from him and puts it on top of the washing machine*)

Sidney: My mistake.

Jane: For someone who's good at some things you're hopeless.

Sidney: Beg your pardon, Admiral, beg your pardon.

Jane puts away the duster and polish.

(*Checking his watch with the clock*) Four and a half minutes to go.

Jane: And you've been at those nuts, haven't you?

Sidney: Nuts?

Jane: In there. In the bowl. On the table. Those nuts. You know the ones I mean.

6

Sidney: I may have had a little dip. Anyway, how did you know I'd been at those nuts? Eh? How did you know, old eagle-eye?

Jane: Because I know how I left them. Now come on, out of my way. Don't start that. I've got things to do.

Sidney: (*closing with her*) What about a kiss then?

Jane: (*trying to struggle free*) Sidney . . .

Sidney: Come on. Christmas kiss.

Jane: Sidney. No, not now. What's the matter with you? Sidney . . . (*She pauses, sniffing*)

Sidney: What's the matter now?

Jane: What's that smell?

Sidney: Eh?

Jane: It's on your tie. What's this smell on your tie?

They both sniff his tie.

There. Can you smell?

Sidney: Oh, that'll be the fly spray.

Jane: Fly spray?

Sidney: Had a bit of a backfire.

Jane: It's killed off your after-shave.

Sidney: (*jovially*) As long as it hasn't killed off my flies, eh. (*He laughs. Suddenly cutting through this*) Eighteen-twenty-eight. Two minutes.

Jane: (*nervous again*) I hope everything's all right. (*She moves over to Sidney and proceeds to brush his jacket in an effort to tidy him up*)

Sidney: When?

Jane: For them. I want it to be right.

Sidney: Of course it's right.

Jane: I mean. I don't want you to be let down. Not by me. I want it to look good for you. I don't want to let you down . . .

Sidney: You never have yet . . .

7

Jane: No, but it's special tonight, isn't it? I mean, with Mr. and Mrs. Brewster-Wright and Mr. and Mrs. Jackson. It's important.
Sidney: Don't forget Dick and Lottie Potter. They're coming too.
Jane: Oh, well, I don't count Dick and Lottie. They're friends.
Sidney: I trust by the end of this evening, we shall all be friends. Just don't get nervous. That's all. Don't get nervous. (*He consults the clock and checks it with his watch*) One minute to go.

A slight pause. The front door chimes sound.

What was that?
Jane: The front door.
Sidney: They're early. Lucky we're ready for them.
Jane: Yes. (*In a sudden panic*) I haven't sprayed the room.
Sidney: All right, all right. You can do it whilst I'm letting them in. Plenty of time.
Jane: It doesn't take a second.

Jane snatches up the air freshener and follows Sidney out into the sitting-room. A silence. Jane comes hurrying back into the kitchen.

Jane puts away the air freshener, removes her pinafore, straightens her clothing and hair in the mirror, creeps back to the kitchen door and opens it a bit. Voices are heard—Sidney's and two others. One is a jolly hearty male voice and one a jolly hearty female voice. They are Dick and Lottie Potter, whom we have the good fortune never to meet in person, but quite frequently hear whenever the door to the kitchen is open. Both have loud, braying distinctive laughs. Jane closes the door, cutting off the voices, straightens her hair and dress for the last time, grips the door handle, takes a deep breath,

8

is about to make her entrance into the room when she sees she is still wearing her bedroom slippers.

Oh.

She takes off her slippers, puts them on the table and scuttles round the kitchen looking for her shoes. She cannot find them. She picks up the slippers and wipes the table with their fluffy side, where they have made a mark.

Oh.

She hurries back to the door, opens it a fraction. Jolly chatter and laughter is heard. Jane stands for a long time, peeping through the crack in the door, trying to catch sight of her shoes. She sees them. She closes the door again. She stands lost.

Oh. Oh. Oh.

The door opens. Loud laughter from off. Sidney comes in laughing. He closes the door. The laughter cuts off abruptly.

Sidney: (*fiercely, in a low voice*) Come on. What are you doing?
Jane: I can't.
Sidney: What?
Jane: I've got no shoes.
Sidney: What do you mean, no shoes?
Jane: They're in there.
Sidney: Where?
Jane: By the fireplace. I left them so I could slip them on.
Sidney: Well, then, why didn't you?
Jane: I didn't have time. I forgot.

Sidney: Well, come and get them.

Jane: No . . .

Sidney: It's only Dick and Lottie Potter.

Jane: You fetch them.

Sidney: I can't fetch them.

Jane: Yes, you can. Pick them up and bring them in here.

Sidney: But I . . .

Jane: Sidney, please.

Sidney: Dear oh dear. What a start. I say, what a start. (*He opens the door cautiously and listens. Silence*) They've stopped talking.

Jane: Have they?

Sidney: Wondering where we are, no doubt.

Jane: Well, go in. Here.

Sidney: What?

Jane: (*handing him her slippers*) Take these.

Sidney: What do I do with these?

Jane: The hall cupboard.

Sidney: You're really expecting rather a lot tonight, aren't you?

Jane: I'm sorry.

Sidney: Yes, well it's got to stop. It's got to stop. I have to entertain out there, you know. (*He opens the door and starts laughing heartily as he does so*)

Sidney goes out, closing the door. Jane hurries about nervously, making still more adjustments to her person and checking her appearance in the mirror. At length the door opens, letting in a bellow of laughter. Sidney returns, carrying Jane's shoes.

(*Behind him*) Yes, I will. I will. I'll tell her that, Dick . . . (*He laughs until he's shut the door. His laugh cuts off abruptly. Thrusting Jane's shoes at her, ungraciously*) Here.

Jane: Oh, thank goodness.

Sidney: Now for heaven's sake, come in.

Jane: (*struggling into her shoes*) Yes, I'm sorry. What did Dick say?

Sidney: When?

Jane: Just now? That you told him you'd tell me.

Sidney: I really can't remember. Now then, are you ready?

Jane: Yes, yes.

Sidney: It's a good job it's only Dick and Lottie out there. It might have been the Brewster-Wrights. I'd have had a job explaining this to them. Walking in and out like a shoe salesman. All right?

Jane: Yes.

Sidney: Right. (*He throws open the door, jovially*) Here she is. (*Pushing Jane ahead of him*) Here she is at last.

Hearty cries of "Ah ha" from Dick and Lottie.

Jane: (*going in*) Here I am.

Jane and Sidney exit.

Sidney: (*closing the door behind him*) At last.

A silence. A long one. Sidney returns to the kitchen. Conversation is heard as he opens and closes the door. He starts hunting round the kitchen opening drawers and not bothering to shut them. After a second, the door opens again, and Jane comes in.

Jane: (*as she enters*) Yes, well you say that to Lottie, not to me. I don't want to know that . . . (*She closes the door*) What are you doing? Oh, Sidney, what are you doing? (*She hurries round after him, closing the drawers*)

Sidney: Bottle-opener. I'm trying to find the bottle-opener. I can't get the top off Lottie's bitter lemon.

11

Jane: It's in there.
Sidney: In there?
Jane: Why didn't you ask me?
Sidney: Where in there?
Jane: On the mantelpiece.
Sidney: The mantelpiece?
Jane: It looks nice on the mantelpiece.
Sidney: It's no use having a bottle-opener on a mantelpiece, is it? I mean, how am I . . . ?

The door chimes sound.

Jane: Somebody else.
Sidney: All right, I'll go. I'll go. You open the bitter lemon. With gin.
Jane: Gin and bitter lemon.
Sidney: And shake the bottle first.

Sidney opens the door. Silence from the room. He goes out, closing it.

Jane: (*to herself*) Gin and bitter lemon—shake the bottle first—gin and bitter lemon—shake the bottle first . . . (*She returns to the door and opens it very slightly. There can now be heard the chatter of five voices. She closes the door and feverishly straightens herself*)

The door opens a crack and Sidney's nose appears. Voices are heard behind him.

Sidney: (*hissing*) It's them.
Jane: Mr. and Mrs. Brewster-Wright?
Sidney: Yes. Ronald and Marion. Come in.

Jane: Ronald and Marion.
Sidney: Come in.

Sidney opens the door wider, grabs her arm, jerks her through the door and closes it.

Jane: (*as she is dragged in*) Gin and bitter lemon—shake the bottle first . . .

Silence. Another fairly long one. The door bursts open and Jane comes rushing out. Murmur of voices.

(*Over her shoulder*) Wait there! Just wait there! (*She dashes to the sink and finds a tea towel and two dish cloths*)

Ronald, a man in his mid-forties, enters. Impressive, without being distinguished. He is followed by an anxious Sidney. Ronald, holding one leg of his trousers away from his body. He has evidently got drenched.

Sidney: Oh dear oh dear. I'm terribly sorry.
Ronald: That's all right. Can't be helped.
Jane: Here's a cloth.
Ronald: Oh, thank you—yes, yes. (*He takes the tea towel*) I'll just use this one, if you don't mind.
Sidney: Well, what a start, eh? What a grand start to the evening. (*With a laugh*) Really, Jane.
Jane: I'm terribly sorry. I didn't realize it was going to splash like that.
Ronald: Well, tricky things, soda siphons. You either get a splash or a dry gurgle. Never a happy medium.
Jane: Your nice suit.
Ronald: Good God, it's only soda water. Probably do it good, eh?

Jane: I don't know about that.

Ronald: (*returning the tea towel*) Thanks very much. Well, it's wet enough outside there. I didn't expect to get wet inside as well.

Sidney: No, no . . .

Jane: Terribly sorry.

Ronald: Accidents happen. Soon dry out. I'll run around for a bit.

Sidney: I'll tell you what. I could let you have a pair of my trousers from upstairs just while yours dry.

Jane: Oh, yes.

Ronald: No, no. That's all right. I'll stick with these. Hate to break up the suit, eh? (*He laughs*)

So do Sidney and Jane.
Marion, a well-groomed woman, a little younger than Ronald and decidedly better preserved, comes in.

Marion: All right, darling?

Ronald: Yes, yes.

Marion: Oh! (*She stops short in the doorway*) Isn't this gorgeous? Isn't this enchanting.

Jane: Oh.

Marion: What a simply dishy kitchen. (*To Jane*) Aren't you lucky.

Jane: Well . . .

Marion: It's so beautifully arranged. Ronnie, don't you agree? Isn't this splendid.

Ronald: Ah.

Marion: Just look at these working surfaces and you must have a gorgeous view from that window, I imagine.

Sidney: Well . . .

Marion: It must be stunning. You must look right over the fields at the back.

Sidney: No—no.

Jane: No, we just look into next door's fence.

14

Marion: Well, which way are the fields?

Jane: I've no idea.

Marion: How extraordinary. I must be thinking of somewhere else.

Sidney: Mind you, we've got a good ten yards to the fence . . .

Ronald: On a clear day, eh?

Sidney: Beg pardon?

Marion: Oh look, Ronnie, do come and look at these cupboards.

Ronald: Eh?

Marion: Look at these, Ronnie. (*Opening and shutting the cupboard doors*) They're so easy to open and shut.

Jane: Drawers—here, you see . . .

Marion: Drawers! (*Opening them*) Oh, lovely deep drawers. Put all sorts of things in these, can't you? And then just shut it up and forget them.

Sidney: Yes, yes, they're handy for that . . .

Marion: No, it's these cupboards. I'm afraid I really do envy you these. Don't you envy them, Ronnie?

Ronald: I thought we had cupboards.

Marion: Yes, darling, but they're nothing like these. Just open and shut that door. It's heaven.

Ronald: (*picking up a booklet from the counter*) Cupboard's a cupboard. (*He sits and reads*)

Jane: (*proudly*) Look. (*Going to the washing machine*) Sidney's Christmas present to me . . .

Marion: (*picking up the air freshener from the top of the washing machine*) Oh lovely. What is it? Hair spray?

Sidney: No, no. That's the fly spray, no. My wife meant the machine. (*He takes the spray from her and puts it down*)

Marion: Machine?

Jane: Washing machine. Here . . .

Marion: Oh, that's a washing machine. Tucked under there. How thrilling. What a marvellous Christmas present.

Jane: Well, yes.

Marion: Do tell me, how did you manage to keep it a surprise from her?

Sidney: Well . . .

Marion: I mean, don't tell me he hid it or wrapped it up. I don't believe it.

Sidney: No, I just arranged for the men to deliver it and plumb it in.

Jane: They flooded the kitchen.

Marion: Super.

Jane: You see, it's the automatic. It's got—all the programmes and then spin-drying and soak.

Marion: Oh, good heavens. Ronnie, come here at once and see this.

Ronald (*reading avidly*) Just coming . . .

Marion (*bending to read the dial*) What's this? Whites—coloureds —my God, it's apartheid.

Jane: Beg pardon?

Marion: What's this? Minimum icon? What on earth is that?

Jane: No, minimum iron.

Marion: Don't tell me it does the ironing too.

Jane: Oh, no, it . . .

Marion: Ronnie, have you seen this extraordinary machine?

Ronald: Yes. Yes . . .

Marion: It not only does your washing and your whites and your blacks and your coloureds and so on, it does your ironing.

Sidney: No, no . . .

Jane: No . . .

Marion: (*to Jane*) We shall soon be totally redundant. (*She picks up the spray and fires it into the air and inhales*) What a poignant smell. It's almost too good to waste on flies, isn't it. Now where . . . ? It's a little like your husband's gorgeous cologne, surely?

Jane: Oh, well . . .

The doorbell chimes.

Marion: Oh, good gracious. What was that? Does that mean your shirts are cooked or something.

Sidney: No, front doorbell.

Marion: Oh, I see. How pretty.

Sidney: Somebody else arrived.

Jane: Yes, I'd better . . .

Sidney: Won't be a minute.

Jane: No, I'll go.

Sidney: No . . .

Jane: No, I'll go.

Jane hurries out, closing the door.

Marion: I do hope your Mr. and Mrs. Potter don't feel terribly abandoned in there. They're splendidly jolly, blooming people, aren't
they?

Sidney: Yes, Dick's a bit of a laugh.

Marion: Enormous. Now, you must tell me one thing, Mr. Hopcraft.
How on earth did you squeeze that machine so perfectly under the
shelf? Did you try them for size or were you terribly lucky?

Sidney: No, I went out and measured the machine in the shop.

Marion: Oh, I see.

Sidney: And then I made the shelf, you see. So it was the right
height.

Marion: No, I mean how on earth did you know it was going to be
right?

Sidney: Well, that's the way I built it.

Marion: No. You don't mean this is you?

Sidney: Yes, yes. Well, the shelf is.

Marion: Ronnie!

Ronald: Um?

Marion: Ronnie, darling, what are you reading?

Ronald: (*vaguely consulting the cover of his book*) Er . . .

Sidney: Ah, that'll be the instruction book for the stove.

Ronald: Oh, is that what it is. I was just trying to work out what I
was reading. Couldn't make head or tail.

17

Marion: Darling, did you hear what Mr. Hop—er . . .
Sidney: Hopcroft.
Marion: Sidney, isn't it? Sidney was saying . . . ?
Ronald: What?
Marion: Darling, Sidney built this shelf on his own. He went out and measured the machine, got all his screws and nails and heaven knows what and built this shelf himself.
Ronald: Good Lord.
Sidney: I've got some more shelves upstairs. For the bedside. And also, I've partitioned off part of the spare bedroom as a walk-in cupboard for the wife. And I'm just about to panel the landing with those knotty pine units, have you seen them?
Marion: Those curtains are really the most insistent colour I've ever seen. They must just simply cry out to be drawn in the morning.

Jane sticks her head round the door.

Jane: Dear—it's Mr. and Mrs. Jackson.
Sidney: Oh. Geoff and Eva, is it? Right, I'll be in to say hallo.
Marion: Geoff and Eva Jackson?
Sidney: Yes. Do you know them?
Marion: Oh yes. Rather. Darling, it's Geoff and Eva Jackson.
Ronald: Geoff and Eva who?
Marion: The Jacksons.
Ronald: Oh, Geoff and Eva Jackson.
Marion: That's nice, isn't it?
Ronald: Yes?
Jane: Are you coming in?
Sidney: Yes, yes.
Marion: Haven't seen them for ages.
Jane: They've left the dog in the car.
Sidney: Oh, good.
Marion: Have they a dog?
Jane: Yes.

Marion: Oh, how lovely. We must see him.
Jane: He's—very big . . .
Sidney: Yes, well, lead on, dear.

Jane opens the door. A burst of conversation from the sitting-room. Jane goes out. Sidney holds the door open for Marion, sees she is not following him and torn between his duties as a host, follows Jane off.

We'll be in here. (*He closes the door*)
Marion: Ronnie . . .
Ronald: (*studying the washing machine*) Mm?
Marion: Come along, darling.
Ronald: I was just trying to work out how this thing does the ironing. Don't see it at all. Just rolls it into a ball.
Marion: Darling, do come on.
Ronald: I think that woman's got it wrong.
Marion: Darling . . .
Ronald: Um?
Marion: Make our excuses quite shortly, please.
Ronald: Had enough, have you?
Marion: We've left the boys . . .
Ronald: They'll be all right.
Marion: What's that man's name?
Ronald: Hopcraft, do you mean?
Marion: No, the other one.
Ronald: Oh, Potter, isn't it?
Marion: Well, I honestly don't think I can sit through many more of his jokes.
Ronald: I thought they were quite funny.
Marion: And I've never had quite such a small gin in my life. Completely drowned.
Ronald: Really? My Scotch was pretty strong.
Marion: That's only because she missed the glass with the soda water. Consider yourself lucky.

19

Ronald: I don't know about lucky. I shall probably have bloody rheumatism in the morning.

Sidney sticks his head round the door. Laughter and chatter behind him.

Sidney: Er—Mrs. Brewster-Wright, I wonder if you'd both . . .
Marion: Oh, yes, we're just coming. We can't tear ourselves away from your divine kitchen, can we, Ronnie? (*Turning to Ronald, holding up the fingers of one hand and mouthing*) Five minutes.
Ronald: Righto.

They all go out, closing the door. Silence. Jane enters with an empty bowl. She hurries to the cupboard and takes out a jumbo bag of crisps and pours them into the bowl. She is turning to leave when the door opens again and Sidney hurries in, looking a little fraught.

Sidney: Tonic water. We've run out.
Jane: Tonic water. Down there in the cupboard.
Sidney: Right.
Jane: Do you think it's going all right?
Sidney: Fine, fine. Now get back, get back there.
Jane: (*as she goes*) Will you ask Lottie to stop eating all these crisps? Nobody else has had any.

Jane goes out closing the door behind her. Sidney searches first one cupboard, then another, but cannot find any tonic.

Sidney: Oh dear, oh dear.

Sidney hurries back to the party closing the door behind him. After a second Jane enters looking worried, closing the door

ACT ONE

*behind her. She searches where Sidney has already searched.
She finds nothing.*

Jane: Oh. (*She wanders in rather aimless circles round the kitchen*)

*Sidney enters with a glass with gin and a slice of lemon in it.
He closes the door.*

Sidney: Is it there?
Jane: Yes, yes. Somewhere . . .
Sidney: Well, come along. She's waiting.
Jane: I've just—got to find it . . .
Sidney: Oh dear, oh dear.
Jane: I tidied them away somewhere.
Sidney: Well, there was no point in tidying them away, was there?
We're having a party.
Jane: Well—it just looked—tidier. You go back in, I'll bring them.
Sidney: Now that was your responsibility. We agreed buying the beverages was your department. I hope you haven't let us down.
Jane: No. I'm sure I haven't.
Sidney: Well, it's very embarrassing for me in the meanwhile, isn't it? Mrs. Brewster-Wright is beginning to give me anxious looks.
Jane: Oh.
Sidney: Well then.

*Sidney goes back in. Jane stands helplessly. She gives a little
whimper of dismay. She is on the verge of tears. Then a sudden decision. She goes to a drawer, reaches to the back and
bring out her housekeeping purse. She opens it and takes out
some coins. She runs to the centre of the room and looks at
the clock.*

Jane: Nineteen-twenty-two. (*Hurried calculation*) Thirteen—fourteen—fifteen—sixteen—seventeen—eighteen—nineteen . . . seven-

21

twenty-two. (*She hurries to the back door and opens it. She holds out her hand, takes a tentative step out and then a hasty step back again. She is again in a dilemma. She closes the back door. She goes to the cupboard just inside the door and, after rummaging about, she emerges holding a pair of men's large wellington boots in one hand and a pair of plimsolls in the other. Mentally tossing up between them, she returns the plimsolls to the cupboard. She slips off her own shoes and steps easily into the wellingtons. She puts her own shoes neatly in the cupboard and rummages again. She pulls out a large men's gardening raincoat. She holds it up, realizes it's better than nothing and puts it on. She hurries back to the centre of the room buttoning it as she does so*) Nineteentwenty-four. (*She returns to the back door, opens it and steps out. It is evidently pelting down. She stands in the doorway holding up the collar of the coat and ineffectually trying to protect her hairdo from the rain with the other hand. Frantically*) Oh . . . (*She dives back into the cupboard and re-emerges with an old hat. She looks at it in dismay. After a moment's struggle she puts it on and hurries back to the centre of the room*) Twenty-five.

Jane returns to the back door, hesitates for a second and then plunges out into the night, leaving the door only very slightly ajar. After a moment, Sidney returns still clutching the glass.

Sidney: Jane? Jane! (*He looks round, puzzled*) Good gracious me. (*He peers around for her*)

Eva comes in. In her thirties, she makes no concessions in either manner or appearance.

Eva: May I have a glass of water?
Sidney: Beg your pardon?
Eva: I have to take these. (*She holds out a couple of tablets enclosed*

in a sheet of tinfoil. She crosses to the back door and stands taking deep breaths of fresh air)

Sidney: Oh, yes. There's a glass here somewhere, I think.

Eva: Thanks.

Sidney: *(finding a tumbler)* Here we are. *(He puts it down on the washing machine)*

Eva stands abstractedly staring ahead of her, tearing the paper round the pills without any effort to open them. A pause. Sidney looks at her.

Er . . .

Eva: What? Oh, thanks. *(She closes the back door and picks up the glass)*

Sidney: Not ill, I hope?

Eva: What?

Sidney: The pills. Not ill?

Eva: It depends what you mean by ill, doesn't it?

Sidney: Ah.

Eva: If you mean do they prevent me from turning into a raving lunatic, the answer's probably yes. *(She laughs somewhat bitterly)*

Sidney: *(laughing, too)* Raving lunatic, yes—*(he is none too certain of this lady)*—but then I always say, it helps to be a bit mad, doesn't it? I mean, we're all a bit mad. I'm a bit mad. *(Pause)* Yes. *(Pause)* It's a mad world, as they say.

Eva: *(surveying the pills in her hand which she has now opened)* Extraordinary to think that one's sanity can depend on these. Frightening, isn't it? *(She puts them both in her mouth and swallows the glass of water in one gulp)* Yuck. Alarming. Do you know I've been taking pills of one sort or another since I was eight years old. What chance does your body have? My husband tells me that even if I didn't need them, I'd still have to take them. My whole mentality is geared round swallowing tablets every three hours, twenty-

23

four hours a day. I even have to set the alarm at night. You're looking at a mess. A wreck. (*She still holds the glass and is searching
round absently as she speaks, for somewhere to put it*) Don't you
sometimes long to be out of your body and free? Free just to float?
I know I do. (*She opens the pedal bin with her foot and tosses the
empty glass into it*) Thanks.

*She puts the screwed up tinfoil into Sidney's hand and starts
for the door. Sidney gawps at her. Eva pauses.*

My God, was that our car horn?
Sidney: When?
Eva: Just now.
Sidney: No, I don't think so.
Eva: If you do hear it, it's George.
Sidney: George?
Eva: Our dog.
Sidney: Oh, yes, of course.
Eva: We left him in the car, you see. We have to leave him in the
   car these days, he's just impossible. He's all right there, usually, but
   lately he's been getting bored and he's learnt to push the horn but-
   ton with his nose. He just rests his nose on the steering-wheel, you
   see.
Sidney: That's clever.
Eva: Not all that clever. We've had the police out twice.
Sidney: A bit like children, dogs.
Eva: What makes you say that?
Sidney: Need a bit of a firm hand now and again. Smack if they're
   naughty.
Eva: You don't smack George, you negotiate terms.
Sidney: Ah. (*He retrieves the glass from the waste-bin*)
Eva: He was only this big when we bought him, now he's grown into
   a sort of yak. When we took him in, he—my God was that me?
Sidney: What?

24

Eva: Did I put that glass in there?

Sidney: Er—yes.

Eva: My God, I knew it, I'm going mad. I am finally going mad. (*She goes to the door and opens it*) Will you please tell my husband, if he drinks any more, I'm walking home.

Sidney: Well, I think that might be better coming from you as his wife.

Eva: (*laughing*) You really think he'd listen to me? He doesn't even know I'm here. As far as he's concerned, my existence ended the day he married me. I'm just an embarrassing smudge on a marriage licence.

Eva goes out, closing the door.

Sidney: Ah. (*He puts the glass on the washing machine and finds Jane's discarded shoes on the floor. He picks them up, stares at them and places them on the draining-board. Puzzled he crosses to the back door and calls out into the night*) Jane! (*He listens. No reply*)

Marion comes in.

Jane!

Marion: I say . . .

Sidney: Rain . . . (*He holds out his hand by way of demonstration, then closes the back door*)

Marion: Oh, yes, dreadful. I say, I think you dashed away with my glass.

Sidney: Oh, I'm so sorry. (*Handing it to her*) Here.

Marion: Thank you. I was getting terribly apprehensive in case it had gone into your washing machine. (*She sips the drink*) Oh, that's lovely. Just that teeny bit stronger. You know what I mean. Not too much tonic . . .

Sidney: No, well . . .
Marion: Perfect.
Sidney: Actually, that's neat gin, that is.
Marion: Oh, good heavens! So it is. What are you trying to do to me? I can see we're going to have to keep an eye on you Mr.—er . . .
Sidney: No, no. You're safe enough with me.
Marion: Yes, I'm sure . . .
Sidney: The mistletoe's in there.
Marion: Well, what are we waiting for? Lead on, Mr.—er . . . (*She ushers him in front of her*)
Sidney: Follow me.

Sidney goes through the door.

Marion: (*as she turns to close it, looking at her watch*) My God.

Marion goes out and closes the door. A pause. Jane arrives at the back door still in her hat, coat and boots. She is soaking wet. She carries a carton of tonic waters. She rattles the back door knob but she has locked herself out. She knocks gently then louder, but no-one hears her. She rattles the knob again, pressing her face up against the glass. We see her mouth opening and shutting but no sound. Eventually, she gives up and hurries away. After a second, Sidney returns. He has the crisp bowl which is again empty. He is about to refill it when he pauses and looks round the kitchen, puzzled and slightly annoyed. He goes to the back door and opens it.

Sidney: Jane! Jane!

Sidney turns up his jacket collar and runs out, leaving the door ajar. As soon as Sidney has gone, the doorbell chimes.

26

ACT ONE

There is a pause, then it chimes again, several times. Ronald enters from the sitting-room.

Ronald: I say, old boy, I think someone's at your front—oh. (*He sees the empty room and the open back door*)

Ronald turns and goes back into the room.

No, he seems to have gone out. I suppose we'd better . . . (*His voice cuts off as he closes the door*)

The doorbell chimes once more. Sidney returns, closing the back door. He finds a towel and dabs his face and hair.

Sidney: Dear oh dear. (*He shakes his head and returns to his crisps. Suddenly, the living-room door bursts open and Jane enters hurriedly in her strange garb, her boots squelching. She shuts the door behind her and stands against it, shaking and exhausted. Sidney turns and throws the bag of crisps into the air in his astonishment.*)
Jane: Oh, my goodness.
Sidney: What are you doing?
Jane: Oh.
Sidney: (*utterly incredulous*) What do you think you're doing?
Jane: (*still breathless*) I went—I went out—to get the tonic. (*She puts a carton of tonic waters on the table*)
Sidney: *Like that?*
Jane: I couldn't find—I didn't want . . .
Sidney: You went out—and came in again, like that?
Jane: I thought I'd just slip out the back to the off-licence and slip in again. But I locked myself out. I had to come in the front.
Sidney: But who let you in?
Jane: (*in a whisper*) Mr. Brewster-Wright.
Sidney: Mr. Brewster-Wright? Mr. Brewster-Wright let you in like that?

27

Jane nods.

What did he say?
Jane: I don't think he recognized me.
Sidney: I'm not surprised.
Jane: I couldn't look at him. I just ran straight past him and right through all of them and into here.
Sidney: Like that?
Jane: Yes.
Sidney: But what did they say?
Jane: They didn't say anything. They just stopped talking and stared and I ran through them. I couldn't very well . . .
Sidney: You'll have to go back in there and explain.
Jane: No, I couldn't.
Sidney: Of course you must.
Jane: Sidney, I don't think I can face them.
Sidney: You can't walk through a respectable cocktail party, the hostess, dressed like that without an apology.
Jane: (*on the verge of tears again*) I couldn't.
Sidney: (*furious*) You take off all that—and you go back in there and explain.
Jane: (*with a wail*) I just want to go to bed.
Sidney: Well, you cannot go to bed. Not at nineteen-forty-seven.
Now, take off that coat.

Jane squelches to the cupboard. Ronald opens the kitchen door. He is talking over his shoulder as he comes in, carrying a glass of Scotch.

Ronald: Well, I think I'd better, I mean . . .
Jane: Oh no.

Jane has had no time to unbutton her coat. Rather than face Ronald, she rushes out of the back door hatless, abandoning

28

her headgear in the middle of the kitchen table. Sidney, try-
ing to stop Jane, lunges after her vainly. The door slams
behind her. Sidney stands with his back to it.

Ronald: (*in the doorway, having caught a glimpse of violent activity,*
but unsure what) Ah, there you are, old chap.

Sidney: Oh, hallo. Hallo.

Ronald: Just popped out, did you?

Sidney: Yes, just popped out.

Ronald: Well—something rather odd. Someone at the door just
now. Little short chap. Hat, coat, boots and bottles. Just stamped
straight through. You catch a glimpse of him?

Sidney: Oh, him.

Ronald: Belong here, does he? I mean . . .

Sidney: Oh, yes.

Ronald: Ah. Well, as long as you know about him. Might have been
after your silver. I mean, you never know. Not these days.

Sidney: No, indeed. No, he—he was from the off-licence. (*He shows*
Ronald the carton)

Ronald: Really?

Sidney: Brought round our order of tonic, you see.

Ronald stares at the hat on the table. Sidney notices and
picks it up.

Silly fellow. Left his hat. (*He picks up the hat, walks to the back*
door, opens it and throws out the hat. He closes the door)

Ronald: Not the night to forget your hat.

Sidney: No, indeed.

Ronald: (*sitting at the table*) Mind you, frankly, he didn't look all
there to me. Wild eyed. That's what made me think . . .

Sidney: Quite right.

Ronald: Ought to get him to come round the back, you know. Take a tip from me. Once you let tradesmen into the habit of using your front door, you might as well move out, there and then.

Sidney: Well, quite. In my own particular business, I always insist that my staff . . .

Ronald: Oh, yes, of course. I was forgetting you're a—you're in business yourself, aren't you?

Sidney: Well, in a small way at the moment. My wife and I. I think I explained . . .

Ronald: Yes, of course. And doing very well.

Sidney: Well, for a little general store, you know. Mustn't grumble.

Ronald: Good to hear someone's making the grade.

Sidney: These days.

Ronald: Quite. (*He picks up the booklet and looks at it*)

A *pause*.

Sidney: I know this isn't perhaps the moment, I mean it probably isn't the right moment, but none the less, I hope you've been giving a little bit of thought to our chat. The other day. If you've had a moment.

Ronald: Chat? Oh, yes—chat. At the bank? Well, yes, it's—probably not, as you say, the moment but, as I said then—and this is still off the cuff you understand—I think the bank could probably see their way to helping you out.

Sidney: Ah well, that's wonderful news. You see, as I envisage it, once I can get the necessary loan, that means I can put in a definite bid for the adjoining site—which hasn't incidentally come on to the market. I mean, as I said this is all purely through personal contacts.

Ronald: Quite so, yes.

Sidney: I mean the site value alone—just taking it as a site—you follow me?

Ronald: Oh, yes.

Sidney: But it is a matter of striking while the iron's hot—before it goes off the boil . . .

Ronald: Mmm . . .

Sidney: I mean, in this world it's dog eat dog, isn't it? No place for sentiment. Not in business. I mean, all right, so on occasions you can scratch mine. I'll scratch yours . . .

Ronald: Beg your pardon?

Sidney: Tit for tat. But when the chips are down it's every man for himself and blow you Jack, I regret to say . . .

Ronald: Exactly.

The sitting-room door opens. Geoffrey enters. Mid-thirties. Good-looking, confident, easy-going. He carries a glass of Scotch.

Geoffrey: Ah. Is there a chance of sanctuary here?

Ronald: Hallo.

Geoffrey: Like Dick Potter's harem in there.

Sidney: Dick still at it?

Geoffrey: Yes. Keeping the ladies amused with jokes . . .

Ronald: Is he? Oh, dear. I'd better—in a minute . . .

Geoffrey: You'll never stop him. Is he always like that? Or does he just break out at Christmas?

Sidney: Oh, no. Dick's a great laugh all the year round . . .

Geoffrey: Is he?

Ronald: You don't say?

Sidney: He's a very fascinating character, is Dick. I thought you'd be interested to meet him. I mean, so's she. In her way. Very colourful. They're both teachers, you know. But he's very involved with youth work of all types. He takes these expeditions off to the mountains. A party of lads. Walks in Scotland. That sort of thing. Wonderful man with youngsters . . .

Ronald: Really?

Sidney: Got a lot of facets.

Ronald: Got a good-looking wife . . .

Sidney: Lottie? Yes, she's a fine-looking woman. Always very well turned out . . .

Geoffrey: Yes, she seems to have turned out quite well.
Sidney: She does the same as him with girls . . .
Ronald: I beg your pardon?
Sidney: Hiking and so on. With the brownies, mainly.
Ronald: Oh, I see.
Geoffrey: Oh.

Pause.

Ronald: Better join the brownies, then, hadn't we? (*He laughs*)
Sidney: (*at length; laughing*) Yes, I like that. Better join the brown-
ies. (*He laughs*) You must tell that to Dick. That would tickle
Dick no end.
Geoffrey: (*after a pause*) Nice pair of legs.
Ronald: Yes.
Sidney: Dick?
Geoffrey: His wife.
Sidney: Lottie? Oh, yes. Mind you, I don't think I've really noticed
them . . .
Geoffrey: Usually, when they get to about that age, they tend to go a
bit flabby round here. (*He pats his thigh*) But she's very trim . . .
Ronald: Trim, oh yes.
Geoffrey: Nice neat little bum . . .
Sidney: Ah.
Ronald: Has she? Hadn't seen that.
Geoffrey: I was watching her, getting up and stretching out for the
crisps. Very nice indeed.
Ronald: Oh, well, I'll keep an eye out.

Pause.

Sidney: That'll be the hiking . . .
Geoffrey: What?

Sidney: (*tapping his thighs; somewhat self-consciously*) This—you know. That'll be the hiking . . .

Ronald: Yes. (*After a pause*) How did you happen to see those?

Geoffrey: What?

Ronald: Her . . . (*He slaps his thighs*) I mean when I saw her just now she had a great big woolly—thing on. Down to here.

Geoffrey: Oh, you can get around that.

Ronald: Really?

Geoffrey: I've been picking imaginary peanuts off the floor round her feet all evening.

Ronald laughs uproariously. Sidney joins in, a little out of his depth.

Ronald: You'll have to watch this fellow, you know.

Sidney: Oh, yes?

Ronald: Don't leave your wife unattended if he's around.

Sidney: Oh, no?

Ronald: Lock her away . . .

Sidney: (*getting the joke at last and laughing*) Ah-ha! Yes . . .

Jane suddenly appears outside the back door, peering in. Sidney waves her away with urgent gestures.

Geoffrey: Still raining, is it?

Sidney: (*holding out his hand*) Yes. Yes.

Ronald: I'll tell you what I've been meaning to ask you . . .

Geoffrey: What's that?

Ronald: Remember that party we were both at—during the summer —Malcolm Freebody's . . . ?

Geoffrey: When was this?

Ronald: Eva—your wife was off sick . . .

Geoffrey: That's nothing unusual.

33

Ronald: I remember it because you were making tremendous head-way with some woman that Freebody was using on his public relations thing . . .

Geoffrey: Was I?

Ronald: Blonde. Sort of blonde.

Geoffrey: (*a short thought*) Binnie.

Ronald: Binnie, was it?

Geoffrey: Binnie something. I think . . .

Ronald: Make out all right, did you?

Geoffrey: Well—you know . . .

Ronald: Really?

Geoffrey: You have no idea. Absolute little cracker. Married to a steward on P. and O. Hadn't seen him for eight months . . .

Ronald: (*chuckling*) Good Lord . . .

Sidney: Ah—ha—oh—ha—ha-ha. (*And other noises of sexual approval*)

The others look at him.

Geoffrey: What have you done with yours? Buried her in the garden?

Sidney: (*guiltily*) What? No, no. She's about. Somewhere.

Geoffrey: Wish I could lose mine, sometimes. Her and that dog. There's hardly room for me in the flat—I mean between the two of them, they have completely reduced that flat to rubble. I mean I'm very fond of her, bless her, she's a lovely girl—but she just doesn't know what it's all about. She really doesn't.

Ronald: Maybe. I still think you're pretty lucky with Eva . . .

Geoffrey: Why's that?

Ronald: Well, she must have a jolly good idea by now about your—er . . .

Geoffrey: Yes. I should imagine she probably has . . .

Ronald: Well, there you are . . .

Geoffrey: Oh now, come off it. Nonsense. She chooses to live with me, she lives by my rules. I mean we've always made that perfectly clear. She lives her life to a certain extent; I live mine, do what I like within reason. It's the only way to do it . . .

Sidney: Good gracious.

Ronald: I wish you'd have a chat with Marion. Convince her.

Geoffrey: Any time. Pleasure.

Ronald: Yes, well, perhaps not—on second thoughts.

Geoffrey: No, seriously. Any man, it doesn't matter who he is—you, me, anyone—(*pointing at Sidney*)—him. They've just got to get it organized. I mean face it, there's just too much good stuff wandering around simply crying out for it for you not . . .

The living-room door opens. Eva appears. Behind, Dick Potter still in full flow, laughing.

(*To Sidney, altering his tone immediately*) Anyway, I think that would be a good idea. Don't you?

Eva: (*coolly*) Are you all proposing to stay out here all night?

Sidney: Oh, dear. We seem to have neglected the ladies.

Eva: Neglected? We thought we'd been bloody well abandoned.

Geoffrey: Can't manage without us, you see.

Eva: We can manage perfectly well, thank you. It just seemed to us terribly rude, that's all.

Geoffrey: Oh, good God . . .

Eva: Anyway. Your jolly friends are leaving.

Sidney: Oh, really. Dick and Lottie? I'd better pop out and see them off, then. Excuse me . . .

Sidney goes off to the sitting-room.

Eva: And, darling, unless you want to see our car towed away again, horn blazing—we'd better get our coats.

Geoffrey: He's not at it again . . .

Eva: Past his supper time . . .

Geoffrey: Oh, honestly, Eva . . .

35

Eva: Don't honestly Eva me, darling. He's your dog.

Geoffrey: What do you mean, he's my dog?

Eva: (*sweetly*) Your house, your dog, your car, your wife—we all belong to you, darling—we all expect to be provided for. Now are you coming, please?

Ronald smiles.

And your wife is looking slightly less than pleased, I might tell you.

Ronald's smile fades. Eva goes out.

Ronald: Oh. (*He looks at his watch*) I suppose I'd better er . . .

Geoffrey: Oh. Ronnie. By the way . . .

Ronald: Mmmm?

Geoffrey: I wondered if you heard anything on the grapevine about the new building Harrison's having put up . . .

Ronald: Oh, this new shopping complex of his.

Geoffrey: Has he got anyone yet?

Ronald: What, you mean in your line?

Geoffrey: Yes. Has he settled on an architect? Or is it still open?

Ronald: Well, as far as I know, it's still wide open. I mean, it's still a gleam in his eye as far as I know.

Geoffrey: Well. If you get a chance to put in a word. I know you're fairly thick with him.

Ronald: Yes, of course. I'll mention it, if the topic comes up. I mean, I'm sure you could do as good a job as anyone.

Geoffrey: Look, I can design, standing on my head, any building that Harrison's likely to want.

Ronald: Yes, well, as I say, I'll mention it.

Geoffrey: I'd be grateful . . .

Marion comes in.

36

Ronald: Ah.

Marion: All right, darling, we're off . . .

Ronald: Right.

Marion: Had a nice time out here?

Ronald: Oh, yes, grand.

Marion: Good. As long as you have . . .

Ronald goes off into the living-room.

This really is a simply loathsome little house. I mean how can people live in them. I mean, Geoff, you're an architect, you must be able to tell me. How do people come to design these sort of monstrosities in the first place, let alone persuade people to live in them?

Geoffrey: Well . . .

Marion: Oh, God. Now he's going to tell me he designed it.

Geoffrey: No. I didn't do it. They're designed like this mainly because of cost and people who are desperate for somewhere to live aren't particularly choosey.

Marion: Oh, come. Nobody can be this desperate.

Geoffrey: You'd be surprised.

Marion: Anyway, it's been lovely to see you. It's been ages. You must come up and see us . . .

Sidney and Ronald, now in his overcoat and carrying Marion's coat, return.

Ronald: Darling . . .

Marion: Sidney, we've had a simply lovely time. Now some time you must come up and see us—and your wife, that's if you ever find her . . .

Sidney: Yes, yes, indeed . . .

37

They all go out, chattering, closing the door. Silence. After a pause, Sidney returns. He closes the door.

(*Rubbing his hands together*) Hah! (*He smiles. Quite pleased. He takes up his drink and sips it. He munches a crisp*)

There is a knock at the back door—rather tentative. It is Jane. Sidney frowns. His concentration is disturbed.

Just a minute. (*He opens the back door*)

Jane falls in—a sodden mass.

(*Recoiling*) My word.
Jane: I saw them leaving.
Sidney: Yes. All gone now. They said for me to say good-bye to you.
Jane: Oh.
Sidney: Where have you been?
Jane: In the garden. Where else? Where do you think?
Sidney: Oh—I don't know. You might have been for a stroll.
Jane: In this?
Sidney: Oh. Still raining, is it?
Jane: Yes. (*Pause*) Sidney, if you'd only explained to them—I could've—I mean I've been out there for ages. I'm soaking . . .
Sidney: Yes. Well, your behaviour made things very difficult. Explanations, that is. What could I say?
Jane: You could have explained.
Sidney: So could you. It was really up to you, wasn't it?
Jane: Yes, I know but—I just thought that you might have—that you would've been . . . (*She gives up*)

Jane starts to peel off her things.

Sidney: All went off rather satisfactorily, anyway . . .

Jane: (*emptying a wellington boot into the sink*) Good—I'm glad . . .

Sidney: So am I. I mean these people just weren't anybody. They are people in the future who can be very, very useful to us . . .

Jane: (*emptying the other boot*) Yes . . .

Sidney: Now, you mustn't do that, Jane. You really mustn't. You see, you get yourself all worked up. And then what happens?

Jane: Yes.

Sidney: Right. Enough said. All forgotten, eh? (*Pause*) Oh dear . . .

Jane: What?

Sidney: We never got round to playing any of our games, did we?

Jane: No.

Sidney: In all the excitement. Never mind. Another year. Well. I think I'll have a look at television. Should be something. Christmas Eve. Usually is. Coming in, are you?

Jane: In a minute . . .

Sidney: Right then.

Sidney goes out closing the door. Jane stands. She sniffs. She has finished putting away her things. Her eye lights on the dirty things scattered about. She picks up a glass or so and puts them in the sink. She picks up the damp cloth and wipes first where the glasses were standing and then slowly, in wider and wider circles, till she has turned it, once more, into a full-scale cleaning operation. As she cleans she seems to relax. Softly at first, then louder, she is heard to sing happily to herself, and—

the curtain falls

End of Act One

ACT TWO

Geoffrey and Eva Jackson's kitchen in their fourth-floor flat. This Christmas.

One door leads to the sitting-room, another into a walk-in cupboard. The room gives an immediate impression of untidiness. It is a room continually lived in, unlike the Hopcraft's immaculate ship's bridge. While it gives signs that the owners have a certain taste for the trendy homespun in both equipment and furnishings, some of the equipment, particularly the gas stove, has seen better days. Besides the stove, the room contains a table (natural scrubbed wood), kitchen chairs (natural scrubbed wood), a chest of drawers (natural scrubbed wood) and a fridge and sink.

When the curtain rises Eva, unmade-up, unkempt and baggy-eyed, sits at the table in her dressing-gown. She is writing with a stub of pencil in a notepad. Whatever it is, it is difficult to word. She and the floor around her are ringed with screwed-up pieces of paper. In front of her is an open scotch bottle. After a minute she tears out the page she has been working on, screws that up as well, and tosses it on the floor to join the others. She starts again.

A door slams. From the sitting-room comes the sound of a large dog barking. Eva looks up alarmed, consults her watch, gives a moan, and quickly closes the notepad to cover up what she has been writing. Geoffrey's voice is heard off.

Geoffrey: (*off*) Darling? Eva—Eva! Quiet, George!

Geoffrey backs in from the sitting-room. George is still bark-ing with wild glee.

George! That's enough, George! Don't be silly, boy. Sit, George. Sit, boy. At once. That's a good boy. Sit. Good George. Good . . .

George has quietened. Geoffrey goes to close the door. George barks with fresh vigour.

George . . . ! (*Giving up*) Oh, all right, suit yourself. (*He closes the door, turning to face Eva for the first time*) Hallo, darling. (*He gives her a kiss as he passes*)

Eva hardly seems to notice. Instead, she sits fiddling with one of her pieces of screwed-up paper. Her face is a tense blank.

God, I need a drink. You want a drink? (*Without waiting for a reply, he takes the scotch, finds a glass and pours himself a drink*) You want one? No? (*He puts the bottle back on the table and drinks*) Cheers. I think we're running into some sort of trouble with the Harrison job. Helluva day. Would you believe I could spend two months explaining to them exactly how to assemble that central-dome. I go along this morning, they're trying to put a bloody great pillar up the middle, straight through the fountain. I said to them, "Listen, you promise to put it up as you're told to—I promise it'll stay up, all right?" I now have to tell Harrison that his super Shopperdrome that he thought was only going to cost so much is going to finish up at twice that. He is not going to be pleased. No, I think I'm in trouble unless I can . . . Oh well, what the hell, it's Christmas. (*Going to the window*) You know, I think it's going to snow. By Boxing Day, that site'll be under six foot of slush, mark my words. That'll put us another six months behind. (*Returning from the window*) Why didn't I pick something simple? (*Seeing the screwed-up paper*) What've you been up to? (*He tries to take Eva's writing pad*)

Eva clings to the pad. Geoffrey shrugs, moves away, then turns and looks at her.

You all right? You're still in your dressing-gown, did you know? Eva? Are you still thinking about this morning? I phoned you at lunch, you know. Were you out? Eva? Oh, come on, darling, we talked it over, didn't we? We were up till four o'clock this morning talking it over. You agreed. You did more than agree. I mean, it was your idea. And you're right. Believe me, darling, you were right. We can't go on. Sooner or later one of us has got to do something really positive for once in our lives—for both our sakes. And it's absolutely true that the best thing that could happen to you and me, at this point in our lives, is for me to go and live with Sally. You were absolutely right. You know I was thinking on the way home—I nipped in for a quick one, that's why I'm a bit late— I was thinking, this could actually work out terribly well. If we're adult about it, I mean. Don't behave like lovesick kids or something. Sally and I will probably get somewhere together—and by that time you'll probably have got yourself fixed up—we could still see each other, you know. What I'm really saying is, let's not go through all that nonsense—all that good-bye, I never want to see you again bit. Because I do want to see you again. I always will. I mean, five years. We're not going to throw away five years, are we? Eva? Eva, if you're sitting there blaming yourself for this in any way, don't. It's me, love, it's all me. It's just I'm—okay, I'm weak, as you put it. I'm unstable. It's something lacking in me, I know. I mean, other men don't have this trouble. Other men can settle down and be perfectly happy with one woman for the rest of their lives. And that's a wonderful thing. Do you think I don't envy that? (*Banging the table*) God, how I envy them that. I mean, do

45

you really think I enjoy living out my life like some sexual Flying Dutchman? Eva, please—please try and see my side just a little, will you? Look, it's Christmas Eve. The day after Boxing Day, I promise—I'll just clear everything of mine that you don't need out of the flat. That way, you can forget I even existed, if that's what you want. But can't we try, between us to make the next couple of days . . . (*He breaks off*) Did I say it's Christmas Eve? Haven't we got some people coming round? Yes, surely we . . . What time did we ask them for? (*He looks at his watch*) Oh, my God. You didn't remember to put them off by any chance, did you? No. Well then . . . Have we got anything to drink in the house? Apart from this? (*He holds up the bottle of scotch*) Oh well, we'll have that for a start. Now then . . . (*He finds a tray, puts it on the table and puts the scotch bottle on the table*) What else have we got? (*He rummages in the cupboards*) Brandy. That'll do. Bottle of coke. Aha, what's this? Tonic wine? Who's been drinking tonic wine? Is that you? Eva? Oh, for heaven's sake, Eva—you've made your point, now snap out of it, will you? We have lots of people coming round who were due five minutes ago. Now come on . . . (*He looks at her and sighs*) O.K. I get the message. O.K. There is no help or co-operation to be expected from you tonight, is that it? All systems shut down again, have they? All right. All right. It won't be the first time—don't worry. (*He returns to his hunt for bottles*) I mean it's not as if you're particularly famous as a gracious hostess, is it? It hasn't been unheard of for you to disappear to bed in the middle of a party and be found later reading a book. (*Producing a couple more bottles—gin and sherry*) I should think our friends will be a little disappointed if you do put in an appearance. (*Finding an assortment of glasses*) When I say our friends, perhaps I should say yours. I will remind you that, so far as I can remember, all the people coming tonight come under the heading of your friends and not mine. And if I'm left to entertain them tonight because you choose to opt out, I shall probably finish up being very, very rude to them. Is that clear? Right. You have been warned. Yes, I know. You're very anxious, aren't you, that I should go and work for the up and coming Mr. Hopcroft? So is up and coming Mr. Hopcroft. But I can tell you both, here and now, I have no intention of helping to perpetrate his squalid little developments. What I lack in morals—I make up in ethics.

Geoffrey stamps out into the sitting-room with the tray.

(*Off, as George starts barking again*) George—no, this is not for you. Get down. I said get down. (*There is a crash as of a bottle coming off the tray*) Oh, really—this damn dog—get out of it . . .

Geoffrey returns with a couple of old coffee-cups which he puts in the sink.

That room is like a very untidy cesspit. (*He finds a dish cloth*) One quick drink that's all they're getting. Then it's happy Christmas and out they bloody well go.

Geoffrey goes out again. He takes with him the dish cloth. Eva opens her notepad and continues with her note. Geoffrey returns. He still has the cloth. In the other hand he has a pile of bits of broken dog biscuit.

Half-chewed biscuit. Why does he only chew half of them, can you tell me that? (*He deposits the bits in the waste bin. He is about to exit again, then pauses*) Eva? Eva—I'm being very patient. Very patient indeed. But in a minute I really do believe I'm going to lose my temper. And we know what happens then, don't we? I will take a swing at you and then you will feel hard done and, by way of reprisal, will systematically go round and smash everything in the flat. And come tomorrow breakfast time, there will be the familiar sight of the three of us, you, me and George, trying to eat our meals off our one surviving plate. Now, Eva, *please* . . .

The doorbell rings. George starts barking.

Oh, my God. Here's the first of them. (*Calling*) George. Now, Eva, go to bed now, please. Don't make things any more embarrassing. (*As he goes out*) George, will you be quiet.

Geoffrey goes out. The door closes. Silence. Eva opens her notepad, finishes her note and tears it out. She pushes the clutter on the table to one side slightly. She goes to a drawer and produces a kitchen knife. She returns to the table and pins the note forcibly to it with the knife. She goes to the window. Geoffrey returns. Barking and chattering are heard in the background—two voices. Eva stands motionless, looking out.

(*Calling back*) He's all right. He's quite harmless. Bark's worse than his bite. (*He closes the door*) It would be the bloody Hopcrofts, wouldn't it. Didn't think they'd miss out. And that lift's broken down, would you believe it. (*Finding a bottle-opener in a drawer*) Every Christmas. Every Christmas, isn't it? Eva, come on, love, for heaven's sake.

Geoffrey goes out, closing the door. Eva opens the window. She inhales the cold fresh air. After a second, she climbs uncertainly onto the window ledge. She stands giddily, staring down and clutching onto the frame. The door opens, chatter, Geoffrey returns, carrying a glass.

(*Calling behind him*) I'll get you a clean one, I'm terribly sorry. I'm afraid the cook's on holiday. (*He laughs*)

The Hopcrofts' laughter is heard. Geoffrey closes the door.

Don't think we can have washed these glasses since the last party. This one certainly didn't pass the Jane Hopcroft Good Housekeep-

48

ing Test, anyway. (*He takes a dish cloth from the sink and wipes the glass rather casually*) I sometimes think that woman must spend . . . Eva! What are you doing?

Eva, who is now feeling sick with vertigo, moans.

Eva! Eva—that's a good girl. Down. Come down—come down— that's a good girl—down. Come on . . . (*He reaches Eva*) That's it. Easy. Come on, I've got you. Down you come. That's it.

He eases Eva gently back into the room. She stands limply. He guides her inert body to a chair.

Come on, sit down here. That's it. Darling, darling, what were you trying to do? What on earth made you want to . . . ? What was the point of that, what were you trying to prove? I mean . . . (*He sees the note and the knife for the first time*) What on earth's this? (*He reads it*) Oh, no. Eva, you musn't think of . . . I mean, what do you mean, a burden to everyone? Who said you were a burden? I never said you were a burden . . .

During the above, Eva picks up the bread-knife, looks at it, then at one of the kitchen drawers. She rises, unseen by Geoffrey, crosses to the drawer and, half opening it, wedges the knife inside so the point sticks out. She measures out a run and turns to face the knife. Geoffrey, still talking, is now watching her absently. Eva works up speed and then takes a desperate run at the point of the knife. Geoffrey, belatedly realizing what she's up to, rushes forward, intercepts her and re-seats her.

Eva, now, for heaven's sake! Come on . . . (*He studies her nervously*) Look, I'm going to phone the doctor. I'll tell him you're very upset and overwrought. (*He backs away and nearly impales*

49

himself on the knife. He grabs it) He can probably give you something to calm you down a bit.

The doorbell rings.

Oh, God, somebody else. Now, I'm going to phone the doctor. I'll
just be two minutes, all right? Now, you sit there. Don't move, just
sit there like a good girl. (*Opening the door and calling off*)
Would you mind helping yourselves? I just have to make one
phone call . . .

*Geoffrey goes out. Silence. Eva finishes another note. A brief
one. She tears it out and weights it down, this time with a tin
of dog food which happens to be on the table. She gazes
round, surveying the kitchen. She stares at the oven. She goes
to it and opens it, looking inside thoughtfully. She reaches inside and removes a casserole dish, opens the lid, wrinkles her
nose and carries it to the draining-board. Returning to the
oven, she removes three shelves and various other odds and
ends that seem to have accumulated in there. It is a very dirty
oven. She looks at her hands, now grimy, goes to the kitchen
drawer and fetches a nearly clean tea towel. Folding it
carefully, she lays it on the floor of the oven. She lies down
and sticks her head inside, as if trying it for size. She is apparently dreadfully uncomfortable. She wriggles about to
find a satisfactory position.*

*The door opens quietly and Jane enters. The hubbub outside
has now died down to a gentle murmur so not much noise
filters through. Jane carries rather carefully two more glasses
she considers dirty. She closes the door. She looks round the
kitchen but sees no-one. She crosses, rather furtively, to the
sink and rinses the glasses. Eva throws an oven tray on to the
floor with a clatter. Jane, startled, takes a step back and gives*

a little squeak. Eva, equally startled, tries to sit up in the oven and hits her head with a clang on the remaining top shelf.

Jane: (*covering*) Mrs. Jackson, are you all right? You shouldn't be on the cold floor in your condition, you know. You should be in bed. Surely? Here . . .

She helps Eva to her feet and steers her back to the table.

Now, you sit down here. Don't you worry about that oven now. That oven can wait. You clean it later. No point in damaging your health for an oven, is there? Mind you, I know just what you feel like, though. You suddenly get that urge, don't you? You say, I must clean that oven if it kills me. I shan't sleep, I shan't eat till I've cleaned that oven. It haunts you. I know just that feeling. I'll tell you what I'll do. Never say I'm not a good neighbour—shall I have a go at it for you? How would that be? Would you mind? I mean, it's no trouble for me. I quite enjoy it, actually—and you'd do the same for me, wouldn't you? Right. That's settled. No point in wasting time, let's get down to it. Now then, what are we going to need? Bowl of water, got any oven cleaner, have you? Never mind, we'll find it—I hope you're not getting cold, you look very peaky. (*Hunting under the sink*) Now then, oven cleaner? Have we got any? Well, if we haven't, we'll just have to use our old friend Mr. Vim, won't we? (*She rummages*)

The door opens: Geoffrey enters and goes to Eva. Conversation is heard in the background.

Geoffrey: Darling, listen, it looks as if I've got . . . (*Seeing Jane*) Oh.
Jane: Hallo, there.

Geoffrey: Oh, hallo—anything you—want?

Jane: I'm just being a good neighbour, that's all. Have you by any chance got an apron I could borrow?

Geoffrey: (*rather bewildered, pointing to the chair*) Er—yes—there.

Jane: Oh, yes. (*Putting it on*) Couldn't see it for looking.

Geoffrey: Er—what are you doing?

Jane: Getting your oven ready for tomorrow, that's what I'm doing.

Geoffrey: For what?

Jane: For your Christmas dinner. What else do you think for what?

Geoffrey: Yes, well, are you sure . . . ?

Jane: Don't you worry about me. (*She bustles around singing loudly, collecting cleaning things and a bowl of water*)

Geoffrey: (*over this, irritated*) Oh, Darling—Eva, look I've phoned the doctor but he's not there. He's apparently out on a call somewhere and the fool of a woman I spoke to has got the address and no number. It'll be quicker for me to try and catch him there than sitting here waiting for him to come back. Now, I'll be about ten minutes, that's all. You'll be all right, will you?

Jane: Don't you fret. I'll keep an eye on her. (*She puts on a rubber glove*)

Geoffrey: Thank you. (*He studies the immobile Eva. On a sudden inspiration, crosses to the kitchen drawer and starts taking out the knives. He scours the kitchen, gathering up the sharp implements*)

Jane watches him, puzzled.

(*By way of explanation*) People downstairs are having a big dinner-party. Promised to lend them some stuff.

Jane: Won't they need forks?

Geoffrey: No. No forks. They're Muslims. (*As he goes to the door*) Ten minutes.

The doorbell rings.

Jane: There's somebody.
Geoffrey: The Brewster-Wrights, probably.
Jane: Oh . . .

Geoffrey goes out, the dog barking as he does so, until the door is closed.

Hark at that dog of yours. Huge, isn't he? Like a donkey—huge. Do you know what Dick's bought him? Dick Potter? He's bought George a Christmas present. One of those rubber rings. You know the ones you throw in the air. One of those. He loves it. He's been running up and down your hallway out there—Dick throwing it, him trying to catch it. But he's really wonderful with dogs, Dick. He really understands them. Do you know he nearly became a dog handler only he didn't have his proper eyesight. But he knows how to treat them. Doesn't matter what sort of dog it is . . . He knows all their ways. (*Turning to the oven*) Now then—oh, this is going to be a big one, isn't it? Dear oh dear. Never mind. Where there's a will. (*Removing the tea towel from the oven*) You haven't been trying to clean it with this, have you? You'll never clean it with this. Good old elbow grease—that's the way. (*She sets to work, her head almost inside the oven*) Shall I tell you something—Sidney would get so angry if he heard me saying this—but I'd far sooner be down here on the floor, on my knees in the oven—than out there, talking. Isn't that terrible. But I'm never at ease, really, at parties. I don't enjoy drinking, you see. I'd just as soon be out here, having a natter with you. (*She starts to sing cheerily as she works, her voice booming round the oven*)

During this, Eva rises, opens the cupboard, pulls out a tin box filled with first-aid things and searches through the contents. Eventually, she finds a white cylindrical cardboard pill box which is what she's looking for. She goes to the sink with it and runs herself a glass of water. She opens the box, takes out a couple of small tablets and puts the box back on the draining-board. She swallows one tablet with a great deal of difficulty and water. The same with the second. She leaves the tap running, pulls the cotton-wool out of the box—and the rest of the pills rattle down the drain. Eva tries desperately to save some with her finger before they can disappear, turning off the tap. This proving ineffective, she tries with a fork. The door opens. Barking and chatter are heard. Sidney enters.

Sidney: Hallo, hallo. Where's everyone gone, then . . . (*Seeing Jane*) Dear oh dear. I just can't believe it. I just can't believe my eyes. You can't be at it again. What are you doing?

Jane: She's under the weather. She needs a hand.

Sidney: Do you realize that's your best dress?

Jane: Oh, bother my best dress.

Sidney: Mr. and Mrs. Brewster-Wright have arrived, you know. Ron and Marion. I hope they don't chance to see you down there. (*Turning to Eva who is still fishing rather half-heartedly with the fork*) And what's the trouble over here, eh? Can I help—since it seems to be in fashion this evening?

Sidney takes the fork from Eva and seats her in her chair.

Now. I'll give you a little tip, if you like. You'll never get a sink unblocked that way. Not by wiggling a fork about in it, like that. That's not the way to unblock a sink, now, is it? All you'll do that way, is to eventually take the chrome off your fork and possibly scratch the plug hole. Not the way. Let's see now . . . (*He runs the tap for a second and watches the water running away*) Yes. It's a little on the sluggish side. Just a little. But it'll get worse. Probably a few tea-leaves, nothing more. Let's have a look, shall we? (*He opens the cupboard under the sink*) Ten to one, this is where your

54

troubles lie. Ah-ha. It's a good old-fashioned one, isn't it? Need the wrench for that one.

Jane: He'll soon fix that for you, won't you, Sidney?

Sidney: Brace of shakes. Shake of braces as we used to say in the Navy. I've got the tools. Down in the car. No trouble at all. (*He turns to Eva*) Nothing serious. All it is, you see—where the pipe bends under the sink there—they call that the trap. Now then. (*He takes out a pencil*) I'll show you. Always useful to know. Paper? (*He picks up Eva's latest suicide note*) This is nothing vital, is it . . . ? Now then. (*He glances curiously at it, then turns it over and starts to draw his diagram on the back*) Now—here's your plug hole, do you see, here—if I can draw it—and this is your pipe coming straight down and then almost doubling back on itself like that, for a second, you see? Then it runs away here, to the drain . . .

Jane: You want to know anything, you ask Sidney . . .

Sidney: And this little bit here's the actual drain trap. And all you have to do is get it open and out it all comes. Easy when you know. Now I suppose I'll have to walk down four flights for my tools. (*He screws up the paper and throws it away. At the door*) Now, don't worry. Lottie's keeping them entertained at the moment and Dick's busy with George, so everybody's happy, aren't they?

Sidney opens the door and goes out. We hear Lottie's laughter and the dog barking distantly for a moment before the door closes.

Jane: It's at times like this you're glad of your friends, aren't you? (*She goes at the oven with fresh vigour, singing cheerily*)

During the above Eva writes another brief note and places it in a prominent position on the table. She now rises and goes to a chair where there is a plastic washing basket filled with

55

clean but unironed clothes. Coiled on top is a washing line.
She returns to the table. Jane, emerging for fresh water,
catches sight of her.

Sorting out your laundry? You're a terror, aren't you? You're worse
than me. (*She returns to her oven and resumes her song*)

Eva begins to pull the washing line from the basket. She
finds one end and ties it in a crude noose. She tests the effec-
tiveness of this on one wrist and satisfied, pulls the rest of
the rope from the basket. Every foot or so is a plastic clothes
peg which she removes.

I think I'm begnning to win through. I think I'm down to the
metal, anyway, that's something. There's about eight layers on
here.

Eva comes across a pair of knickers and two pairs of socks
still pegged to the line. She removes these and replaces them
in the basket.

There's something stuck on the bottom here like cement. You
haven't had cement for dinner lately, have you? (*She laughs*)

Eva now stands with her clothes line gazing at the ceiling.
There are two light fittings and her eyes rest on the one im-
mediately above the table. She crosses to the door, clicks a
switch and just this one goes out.

Whooo! Where was Moses . . . ? What's happened? Bulb gone,
has it? We'll get Sidney to fix that when he comes back. Keep him
on the go. (*She returns to the oven again, changing her tune to*
something suitable like "Dancing in the Dark")

Eva climbs first onto a chair then onto the table holding her rope. She removes the bulb and shade in one from the socket and places them on the table at her feet. She is beginning to yawn more and more frequently and is obviously beginning to feel the effect of the sleeping pills. Swaying slightly, she starts to tie the rope round the socket. This proves a difficult operation since she has far too much rope for the job. She finally manages a knot which loosely encircles it. She gives the rope a gentle tug—it holds. She tries again. It still remains in position. She gives it a third tug for luck. The rope slides down and pulls the socket away from the wires. The holder clatters onto the table and she is left clutching the rope. She stands swaying more pronouncedly now, a faint look of desperation on her face. Ronald enters. Behind him we hear Lottie Potter's laughter and, more distant, a dog barking.

Ronald: Now then, how's our little invalid getting . . . (*Seeing Eva*) Oh, good God. (*He dashes forward and steadies Eva*) My dear girl, what on earth are you doing up there?

Jane (*emerging from her oven*) Oh, no. She's a real terror, you know. (*She goes to assist Ronald in helping Eva off the table and back on to a chair*) She can't keep still for a minute. (*Reprovingly to Eva*) You could have hurt yourself up there, you silly thing.

Ronald folds up the rope, which is looped around Eva's wrist, and leaves it in her hand.

Ronald: Lucky I . . .
Jane: Yes, it was.
Ronald: I mean. What was she trying to do?
Jane: Bulb's gone.
Ronald: (*looking up*) Yes, so it has. Well, you could have asked me

to do that, you know. I'm no handyman but even I can change a bulb.

Sidney enters with a large bag of tools. Behind him we hear Lottie's laughter and a dog barking.

Sidney: Here we are, back again. I've brought everything, just in case. Everything except the kitchen sink and that's already here, eh? (*He laughs*)

Ronald: What? Oh, yes. Very good.

Jane (*amused*) Except the kitchen sink. Honestly.

Sidney: (*noticing the light*) Hallo, hallo. More trouble? (*He puts the tool bag by the sink*)

Ronald: Nothing much. Just a bulb gone.

Sidney: You've lost more than a bulb, by the look of it. You've lost the whole fitting.

Ronald: Good gracious me. So we have. Look at that.

Sidney: Just the bare wires, you see.

Ronald: Yes. There's no thingummyjig.

Jane: Just the wires, aren't there?

Sidney: Don't like the look of that.

Ronald: No.

Jane: No.

Sidney: I mean, if that was to short across like it is . . .

Ronald: Yes.

Jane: Yes.

Sidney: You could finish up with a fuse, or a fire . . .

Ronald: Or worse.

Jane: Worse.

Sidney: I mean, you've only got to be carrying, say, for instance, a pair of aluminum steps across the room and you happen accidentally to knock against the wires, electricity would be conducted down the steps and straight into you. Natural earth, you see. Finish.

Ronald: I suppose that would go for a very tall man in, say, a tin hat, eh? (*He laughs*)

Sidney: True, true. Not so probable. But true.

Jane: Lucky it's not the war time.

Sidney: Oh, yes. In certain cases, one touch could be fatal.

Ronald: Better fix it, I suppose.

Sidney: I'd advise it. Going to have a go, are you?

Ronald: Well—I don't know. Looks a bit technical for me.

Sidney: Oh, no. Very simple. Nothing to it. Look, you've got your two wires coming down . . . Look, I'll draw it for you. (*He whips out his pencil again and, searching for a piece of paper, picks up Eva's suicide note. With a casual glance at it*) Nothing important this, is it? (*Without waiting for a reply, he turns it over and starts to sketch*)

Eva stares—fascinated.

You've got your two wires coming down here, you see—like that. They go through the top of the plug, here—excuse the drawing, and then they just screw into the little holes on the prongs, you see? Tighten your grubs. Screw your top to your bottom and away you go.

Ronald: Let there be light.

Sidney: Exactly.

Eva scrawls another note.

Ronald: Oh, well, that looks—simple enough. (*He still seems doubtful*)

Sidney: Right. I'll get you a screwdriver and I'll get going on the sink. (*Opening his tool bag*) Now then, let's get you fixed up. What've we got here? (*He rummages through his tools, taking out a screwdriver and a spare fitting*)

Ronald: Good gracious. What a collection.

Sidney: This is just the set I keep in the car.
Ronald: Really? Get a lot of trouble with it, do you?

During the above Eva climbs slowly on to her chair, steps on to the table and reaches out with both hands towards the bare wires. Jane, who has returned to her oven, turns in time to see her.

Jane: Watch her!
Sidney: Hey-hey . . .
Ronald: Hoy . . .

All three of them run, grab Eva and pull her back in the chair.

Sidney: They might have been live.
Ronald: Yes. (*A thought*) Might they?
Sidney: Yes.
Ronald: Well, how do we know they're not?
Sidney: Check the switches first.
Ronald: Yes, well, don't you think we'd better? I mean, I'm going to be the one who . . .
Sidney: (*striding to the door*) Check the switches, by all means.

Sidney plays with both switches, plunging the room into darkness a couple of times.

Jane: (*during this, still with Eva*) She's got a charmed life, honestly. The sooner that doctor gets here . . .
Ronald: He'll fix her up.
Jane: He'd better.
Sidney: (*completing his check*) Yes, all safe. (*He takes off his jacket and puts it over the back of a chair*)
Ronald: Ah.

Sidney: Should be, anyway. Unless they've put this switch on upside down, of course.

Ronald: How do we know they haven't?

Sidney: Well, you'll be the first to find out, won't you? (*He roars with mirth*)

Jane: (*equally tickled*) You'll be the first . . .

Ronald is less amused.

Sidney: Well, let's get down to it, shall we?

Ronald: (*gazing at the light*) Yes.

Sidney: Each to his own. (*He starts work under the sink*)

Jane: Each to his own. (*She returns to the oven*)

They prepare for their various tasks.

This is coming up a treat.

Sidney: Ought to get—er—Marion out here, eh? Find her something to do.

Ronald: (*clearing the things off the table*) No—no. I don't think she'd contribute very much. Probably better off with the Potters. Matter of fact, she's just a bit—on her pins. You know what I mean.

Sidney: Ah, well. Christmas.

Jane: If you can't do it at Christmas . . .

Sidney: Once a year, eh?

Ronald: Not in my wife's case. Festive season recurs rather more frequently. Every three or four days.

Sidney: (*under the sink*) Ah-ha! You're going to be a tricky little fellow, aren't you? Nobody's opened you since you were last painted.

Sidney clatters under the sink. Jane scrubs cheerfully on. Ronald sets to work, standing on the table and on Eva's lat-

est note. He tackles his own particular job extremely slowly and with many false starts. He is not particularly electrically-minded. Eva attempts, under the following, to rescue her note from under Ronald's feet. It rips. She scrawls another rapidly.

Ronald: Must be pretty pleased with your year, I should imagine.
Sidney: Beg pardon?
Ronald: Had a good year. Must be pretty pleased.
Sidney: Oh, yes. Had a few lucky hunches. Seemed to pay off.
Ronald: I should say so.
Sidney: Mustn't complain, anyway.
Jane: No. Mustn't complain.
Sidney: As long as you're looking after our money. Eh? (*He laughs*)
Ronald: Oh, yes. Yes.

They work. Sidney whistles. Ronald hums. Jane sings. Occasionally, the workers break off their respective melodies to make those sounds that people make when wrestling with inanimate objects. "Come on, you little . . . Just one more . . . get in, get in, etc." During this Eva, having finished her note, sees Sidney's bag of tools. Unseen by the others, she goes to the bag and removes a lethal-looking tin of paint stripper. Also a hammer and a nail. She nails her latest note to the table with the hammer which she leaves on the table. Turning her attention to the paint stripper, she tries to get the top off. It is very stiff. She struggles vainly then goes to the room door, intending to use it as a vice.

At this moment Marion enters. Eva is pushed behind the door, and, as it swings shut, she clings to the handle and falls across the floor. While the door is open the dog barks and raised voices are heard.

Marion: (*holding a gin bottle and glass*) I say—something rather ghastly's happened.
Ronald: (concentrating hard) Oh, yes?
Marion: Goodness! Don't you all look busy? Darling, what are you doing up there?

Eva tries to open the bottle with the walk-in cupboard door.

Ronald: Oh, just a little light electrical work or should I say a little electrical light work? (*He laughs*)
Sidney: Electrical light work. (*He laughs*)
Jane: Electrical light work. (She laughs)
Sidney: I like that—yes . . .
Marion: Yes, very funny, darling. Now do come down, please, before you blow us all up. You know absolutely nothing about that sort of thing at all.
Ronald: I don't know . . .
Marion: Absolutely nothing.
Ronald: I fixed that bottle lamp with a cork in it, didn't I?
Marion: Yes, darling, and we all had to sit round admiring it while the lampshade burst into flames.

Eva goes to the toolbag for a screwdriver.

Ronald: (*irritably*) That was entirely the fault of the bloody lampshade.
Marion: I was terrified. The whole thing was an absolute death trap. I had to give it to the Scouts for jumble.
Sidney: What was the trouble?
Marion: It was like modern sculpture. Bare wires sticking out at extraordinary angles.

Eva goes and sits down in a corner.

63

Sidney: No. I meant when you came in.

Marion: Oh, yes. What was it? Something awful. (*She remembers*) Oh, yes. I came for help, that's right. That dog . . .

Jane: George?

Marion: Is that his name—George—yes. Well, he's just bitten that Potter man in the leg.

Jane: Oh, dear.

Marion: Terribly nasty. Right through his trousers. Of course, it was entirely his fault. I mean, he was leaping about being desperately hearty with the poor animal till it had froth simply foaming from its jowls and didn't know where it was.

Jane: Oh, dear, are they . . . ?

Sidney: Yes, what are they . . . ?

Marion: Well, I think they were thinking of going. If they haven't gone. They seem to think he might need an anti-something.

Sidney: Rabies.

Marion: Probably. I'll see. (*She opens the door*)

Silence.

(*Calling*) I say, hallo. Hallo there.

There is a low growl.

Oh, dear.

Ronald: What's the matter?

Marion: It's sort of crouching in the doorway chewing a shoe and looking terribly threatening.

Ronald: Really?

Marion: I don't think it's going to let us through, you know.

Ronald: (*picking up the tin of dog meat and moving tentatively to the sitting-room*) He's probably all right, he just needs calming down. Here, boy, boy, good boy. Hallo, boy, good boy.

64

A growl. Ronald returns, closes the door, and goes back to his work.

No, well, best to leave them when they're like that. Just a bit excited.

Sidney: Mind you, once they've drawn blood, you know . . .

Jane: Old Mr. Allsop's Alsatian . . .

Sidney: Yes.

Marion: Yes. Well, it's lucky I brought the drink. Keep the workers going. And the invalid. How is she?

Ronald: Very groggy.

Marion: (*peering at her*) Golly, yes. She's a dreadful color. How are you feeling?

Jane: I don't think she really knows we're here.

Marion: Hallo. Hallo, there . . . (*No response*) No, you're right. She's completely gone. Poor thing. Oh well, drink, everyone?

Jane: Not just at the moment. Nearly finished.

Marion: Jolly good. (*Nudging Sidney with her leg*) What about you?

Sidney: In a moment. In just a moment.

Ronald: Darling, I wouldn't drink too much more of that.

Marion: Oh, Ronnie, don't be such a misery. Honestly, he's such a misery. He's totally incapable of enjoying a party.

Ronald: No, all I'm saying is . . .

Marion: Well, Eva and I'll have one, won't we, Eva?

Marion pours out two glasses.

Sidney: (*from under the sink*) Ah!

Jane: All right?

Sidney: Got it off.

Jane: Oh, well done.

Marion: What's he got off?

65

Eva finally gets the lid off the paint stripper and is about to drink it.

Sidney: That was a wrestle and no mistake. But I got it off. The big question now is, can I get it on again.

Marion: Eva, dear, now you drink that. (*She puts the glass in Eva's hand, removing the tin of stripper*) That'll do you far more good than all the pills and patent medicines put together. (*She puts the paint stripper on the draining-board*)

Ronald: Marion, seriously, I wouldn't advise . . .

Marion (*hitting him on the foot with the gin bottle*) Oh, Ronnie, just shut up!

Ronald: Ah!

Marion: (*to Eva; confidentially*) You'd never think it but he was a really vital young man, Eva. You'd never think it to look at him, would you?

Marion fills Eva's glass of gin so that she is forced in her inert state to drink some.

Sidney: (*emerging from his sink*) Well, time for a break. Now then, did somebody promise a drink?

Marion: (*pushing the bottle towards him*) Help yourself.

Sidney: Thank you.

Jane: I think that's about as much as I can do. It's a bit better.

Marion: (*going to the stove*) Oh, look, isn't that marvellous. Look at that splendid oven.

Sidney: Well done. Well done.

Jane: Bit of a difference. (*She picks up her bowl of water and carries it to the sink*)

Ronald: (*having difficulty*) Ah . . .

Sidney: How's the electrical department?

Ronald: (*muttering*) Damn fiddly thing.

Sidney: (*seeing Jane*) Hey! Don't pour that down now!

66

Jane: Oh. Nearly forgot.

Sidney: You'd have been popular. (*He puts the gin bottle on the table*)

Jane: I'd have been popular.

Marion: Well, I'm just going to sit here all night and admire that oven. I think she's honestly better than our Mrs. Minns, isn't she, darling?

Ronald: Anyone's better than our Mrs. Minns.

Marion: Oh, she means well. We have our Mrs. Minns. She's a dear old soul. She can hardly see and she only comes in for two hours a day and when she's gone we spend the rest of the time cleaning up after her. But she's got an absolute heart of gold.

Ronald: Largely paid for by us.

Sidney: Good health. Happy Christmas to all.

Marion: Happy New Year.

Jane: Yes.

Sidney: Get this lot finished, maybe there'll be time for a game . . .

Jane: Oh, yes . . .

Marion: What sort of game do you mean?

Sidney: You know. Some good party game. Get everyone jumping about.

Marion: What an obscene idea.

Sidney: Oh, they're great fun. We've had some laughs, haven't we?

Jane: Talk about laughs . . .

Ronald: Blast.

Sidney: What's the matter?

Ronald: Dropped the little thing. Could you see if you can see it. I've got to keep holding on to this or it'll drop off. Little thing about so big.

Marion: What little thing?

Ronald: A whajamacallit.

Jane: Small was it?

Ronald: Lord, yes. Tiny little thingy.

Sidney: Oh dear oh dear.

67

They hunt, Sidney crawls on hands and knees.

Jane: Might have rolled anywhere.

Marion: What are we looking for?

Ronald: Little whosit. Goes in here.

Marion: Darling, do be more precise. What's a whosit?

Jane: You know, one of those—one of those—isn't that silly I can't think of the word.

Marion: Well, I refuse to look till I know what we're looking for. We could be here all night. I mean, from the look of this floor it's simply littered with little whosits.

Sidney: (*under the table*) Can't see it.

Jane: It's on the tip of my tongue . . . that's it, a nut. Little nut.

Marion: (*searching by the sink*) Oh, well then, a nut. Now we know. Everyone hunt for a little nut.

Eva goes and sits at the table.

Sidney: I didn't know we were looking for a nut.

Jane: Aren't we?

Ronald: No. A screw. That's what I'm after, a screw.

Sidney: A screw, yes.

Jane: Oh, a screw.

Marion: All right, everybody, stop looking for nuts. Ronnie's now decided he wants a screw. I can't see a thing, and I think it would be terribly sensible if we put the light on, wouldn't it?

Ronald: Good idea.

Marion goes to the light switch.

Sidney: (*realizing far too late*) No, I wouldn't turn that on . . .

Marion presses the switch.

68

Marion: There.

Ronald, on the table, starts vibrating, emitting a low moan.

Sidney: (*rising*) Turn it off.
Jane: Get him away.
Marion: Darling, what on earth are you doing?
Jane: (*reaching out to pull Ronald away*) Get him away.
Sidney: No, don't touch him, he's live. (*He goes to the switch*)

Jane touches him and recoils, with a squeak.

Ronald: (*through gritted teeth*) Somebody turn it off.

Sidney turns it off.

Sidney: All right. Panic over.

Ronald continues to vibrate.

Jane: Turn him off, Sidney.
Sidney: I have.
Jane: Turn him off!
Sidney: He is off. (*Calming Jane*) Now, pull yourself together. Help me get him down. Get him down.

Sidney and Jane guide Ronald down from the table and guide him to a chair. Marion watches them.

Marion: Good Lord. Wasn't that extraordinary?
Sidney: Easy now.
Jane: Take it slowly.

Eva pours herself another drink.

Marion: Whenever he fiddles about with anything electrical it always ends in disaster. This always happens. Is he all right?

Sidney: He's in a state of shock.

Jane: He would be.

Sidney: Sit him down and keep him warm—that's the way. Pass me my jacket. Jacket. Jacket.

Marion: He looks frightfully odd.

Jane: (bringing Sidney's jacket) Here.

Sidney: He needs more. He really needs to be wrapped up, otherwise . . .

Jane: (looking round) There's nothing much here.

Sidney: Well, find something. In the other room. We need blankets.

Jane: Right.

Jane goes to the door while Marion looks vaguely round the kitchen.

Sidney: Now easy, old chap. Just keep breathing . . .

Jane opens the door. There is a fierce growling. She withdraws swiftly and closes it.

Jane: He's still there.

Sidney: Who?

Jane: The dog.

Sidney: Well, step over him. This is an emergency.

Jane: I'm not stepping over him. You step over him.

Sidney: Oh dear oh dear.

Marion: (who has found the washing basket) What about these bits and bobs? (She picks up an article of clothing)

Sidney: What's that?

Marion: Last week's washing, I think. (Sniffing it) It seems fairly clean. Might be better than nothing.

Sidney: Yes, well, better than nothing.

Marion: It seems dry.

Jane: Better than nothing.

> *Between them, they cover Ronald in an assortment of laundry, both male and female. He finishes up more or less encased in it but still quivering.*

Sidney: Quick as you can. Come along, quick as you can.

Jane: (*examining a shirt*) She hasn't got this collar very clean.

Sidney: Jane, come along.

Marion: (*holding up a petticoat*) Oh, that's rather pretty. I wonder where she got this.

Sidney: Not the time for that now. That the lot?

Marion: Yes. Only socks left, And you-know-whats.

Sidney: Well, it'll keep his temperature up.

Marion: Oh, my God, what does he look like? Ronnie! You know I've got a terrible temptation to phone up his chief cashier. If he could see him now . . . (*She starts to laugh*)

Jane: I don't think he's very well, you know.

Marion: Yes, I'm sorry. It's just that I've never seen anything quite so ludicrous.

Sidney: (*moving a chair up beside Ronald*) Might I suggest that Marion sits down with her husband just until the doctor gets here for Mrs. Jackson . . .

Jane: Then he can look at them both.

Sidney: Precisely.

Jane: Lucky he was coming.

Sidney: Yes, well, we'd better just finish off and clear up, hadn't we?

Marion: (*sitting beside Ronald*) Would you like a drink, darling? You look dreadful!

Jane: I'd better just go over the floor.

Sidney: (*preparing to go under the sink again*) No, dear, we don't want you to go over the floor. Not now . . .

Jane: Just where we've been tramping about. If Doctor's coming. It won't take a minute.

Sidney: All right. Carry on, Sister. Sorry I spoke.
Jane: (*going to the walk-in cupboard*) Now where does she keep her broom?
Ronald: (*strained tone*) You know, I feel very peculiar.

Jane finds the broom and starts clearing the immediate vicinity around the table.

Marion: Well, I hope you won't be like this all over Christmas, darling. I mean we've got your mother over tomorrow for lunch and Edith and the twins on Boxing Day—I just couldn't face them alone, I just couldn't.
Jane: (*to Eva*) Excuse me, dear. I wonder if you could just . . . (*She winds up the rope, still looped to Eva's wrist, and puts it in Eva's hand*) Tell you what, why don't you sit up here? Just for a second. Then I won't get in the way of your feet. (*She assists Eva to sit on the edge of the table*) Upsidaisy.
Sidney: (*sliding under the sink*) She all right still?
Jane: I think so.

Eva yawns.

Just a bit tired. Neglected you in all the excitement, haven't we? Never mind. Just sit there. Doctor'll be here soon. (*She sweeps under the table*)
Marion: You know, I believe I'm beginning to feel dizzy as well. I hope I haven't caught it from her.
Jane: I hope not. What a Christmas, eh?
Sidney: (*from under the sink*) We'll be laughing about this.
Jane: (*going to the sink and lifting Sidney's feet*) Excuse me, dear. What's that?
Sidney: I say, in about two weeks' time, we'll——

Jane pours the water away in the sink.

—all be sitting down and laughing about—aaaah!
Jane: Oh, no.
Sidney: Put the plug in.
Jane: (*feverishly following the plug chain*) I can't find the end.
Sidney: Put the plug in!
Jane: (*putting the plug in*) I'm sorry.
Sidney: (*emerging from under the sink, his top half drenched in dirty water*) Look what you've done.
Jane: I'm terribly sorry. (*She picks up a dish cloth*)
Sidney: Look what you have done! You silly woman!

She tries to mop him down with the dish cloth.

(*Beating her away*) Don't do that! Don't do that! It's too late for that. Look at this shirt. This is a new shirt.
Jane: Well, it'll wash. It'll wash. I'll wash it. It's only oven grease.
Sidney: I told you, didn't I? I said, whatever you do—don't pour water down there, didn't I?
Jane: I didn't think . . .
Sidney: Obviously.
Jane: Well, take the shirt off now and I'll . . .
Sidney: And I'll go home in my singlet, I suppose?
Jane: Nobody'll notice.
Sidney: Of course they'll notice. Otherwise, there'd be no point in wearing a shirt in the first place, would there? If nobody noticed, we'd all be walking around in our singlets.
Jane: It's dark.
Sidney: Don't change the subject. It would really teach you a lesson if I caught pneumonia.
Jane: (*tearful*) Don't say that.
Sidney: Teach you, that would.

Jane sniffs. Sidney strides to the door.

Dear oh dear.
Jane: (*following him*) Where are you going?

73

Sidney: To get my overcoat before I freeze. Where else do you think
I'm going?
Jane: But, Sidney . . .

*Sidney ignores her, flinging open the door and striding out,
making a dignified exit. There is a burst of furious barking.
Sidney reappears very swiftly and closes the door behind him.*

Sidney: (*to Eva; furiously*) That dog of yours is a liability. You
ought to keep that animal under control. I can't even get to my
overcoat. It's not good enough.

Eva slowly lies down on the kitchen table, oblivious.

Jane: Come and sit down.
Sidney: Sit down? What's the point of sitting down?
Jane: Geoff should be back soon.
Sidney: I should hope so. This isn't what you expect at all. Not when
you come round for a quiet drink and a chat. (*Almost screaming in
Eva's ear*) This is the last time I accept hospitality in this house-
hold.
Jane: Ssh.
Sidney: What?
Jane: She'll hear you.
Sidney: I don't care who hears me. (*He sits*)
Jane: Ssh. (*She sits*)

*A pause. The four of them are sitting. Eva lies. Ronald con-
tinues to look glassy, quivering slightly; Marion's drinking
has caught up with her. Jane looks abjectly miserable. Sidney
shivers in his vest.*

Sidney: And we're missing the television.
Jane: Ssh.

74

Act Two

A silence. Then, from apparently nowhere, a sleepy voice begins to sing dreamily. It is Eva.

Eva: (*singing*) "On the first day of Christmas my true love sent to me, a partridge in a pear tree. On the second day of Christmas my true love sent to me, two turtle doves——

Marion: (*joining her*)—and a partridge in a pear tree. On the third day of Christmas my true love sent to me, three French hens——

Jane: (*joining her*)—two turtle doves and a partridge in a pear tree. On the fourth day of Christmas my true love sent to me, four calling birds——

Ronald: (*joining them*)—three French hens, two turtle doves and a partridge in a pear tree.

All: On the fifth day of Christmas my true love sent to me five gold rings, etc.

As the bedraggled quintet begin to open up, the singing gets bolder and more confident. Somewhere in the distance George begins to howl. Eva, still lying on her back, conducts them dreamily with both hands and then finally with the hammer. The door bursts open. Geoffrey enters hurriedly, calling behind him.

Geoffrey: Through here, Doctor. Please hurry, I . . .

Geoffrey is suddenly aware of the sound behind him. He turns, still breathless from his run up four flights. His mouth drops further open as he surveys the scene. The singing continues unabated, as the lights black-out and—

the curtain falls

End of Act Two

ACT THREE

The Brewster-Wright's kitchen. Next Christmas.

They live in a big old Victorian house, and the kitchen, though modernized to some extent, still retains a lot of the flavor of the original room. A sink, an electric stove, a fridge, a dark wood sideboard, a round table and chairs form the substantial furnishings for the room. On the table is an elderly radio set. There is a door, half of opaque glass, to the hall, and a garden door.

When the curtain rises, Ronald is sitting in an armchair near the table. He wears a scarf and a green eye-shade. Beside him is a lighted portable oil stove. At his elbow is an empty teacup. The radio is on, playing very quietly a jolly carol. Ronald is reading a book. He is obviously enjoying it, for every two or three seconds he chuckles to himself out loud. This continues for some seconds, until the door from the hall opens and Eva enters. She wears a winter coat and carries an empty teacup and a plate, which she puts down on the draining-board.

Ronald: Oh. Hallo there.
Eva: All right?
Ronald: Oh, yes. (*He switches off the radio*)
Eva: Are you warm enough in here?
Ronald: Oh, yes. It's fine in here. Well, not too bad.
Eva: The rest of the house is freezing. I don't envy you going to bed.
Ronald: Her room's all right, though, is it?
Eva: Oh, she's got three electric fires blazing away.

Ronald: My God. That'll be the second power station I've paid for this winter.

Eva: She seems to be rather dug in up there. Almost in a state of hibernation. Doesn't she ever come out?

Ronald: Not if she can help it. Heating system went on the blink, you see—usual thing and we had a few frosty words over it and—the outcome was, she said she wasn't setting foot outside her room until I got it fixed.

Eva: (*putting on a pair of gloves*) Well, how long's it been like this?

Ronald: (*vaguely*) Oh, I don't know. Two or three weeks, I suppose.

Eva: Well, that's disgusting. Can't you get the men round to fix it?

Ronald: Yes, yes. I have phoned them several times. But I've been a bit unlucky up to now. They always seem to be at lunch . . .

Eva: (*taking off her coat and putting it on the back of a chair*) Well, I wouldn't put up with it. I'd scream the place down till Geoffrey got it fixed. (*She hunts in the cupboards*)

Ronald: Yes, we've had a packet of trouble with this central heating. Always goes on the blink. Either the day before Christmas, the day before Easter or the day before Whitsun. Always seems to manage it. Don't understand the principle it works on but whatever it is, seems to be very closely tied in with the Church calendar. (*He laughs*) Can I help you at all?

Eva: She said she'd like a sandwich. (*She puts a plate, knife, bread and a jar of peanut butter on a bread board*)

Ronald: (*looking at his watch*) Oh, yes. She's about due for a sandwich.

Eva: I'm looking for the butter.

Ronald: Oh, don't you bother to do that, I'll . . .

Eva: It's all right. Where do you keep your butter?

Ronald: Do you know, that's very interesting. I have absolutely no idea. A closely guarded secret kept by Mrs. Minns. I suppose we could hazard a guess. Now then, butter. Try the fridge.

Eva: Fridge?

Ronald: Keeps it soft. It's warmer in there than it is outside.

Eva: (*looking in the fridge*) Right first time. (*She sets about making a sandwich, taking off one glove*)

Ronald: What's she want? Peanut butter?

Eva: Apparently.

Ronald: Good grief. She's got an absolute craving for that stuff lately. That and cheese footballs. All most alarming. She's not up there knitting little blue bootees, by any chance?

Eva: Not that I noticed.

Ronald: Thank God for that.

Eva: She looks a lot better than when I last saw her, anyway.

Ronald: Really? Yes, yes. Well, she got a bit overtired, I think. Principally.

Eva: Geoff'll be here in a minute to pick me up. I'll get out of your way. I just heard Marion was—I hope you didn't mind . . .

Ronald: No, very good of you to look round. Sure she appreciated it. She doesn't get many visitors. Lottie Potter looked in briefly. That set her back a couple of weeks. No, the trouble with Marion you see, is she lives on her nerves. Far too much.

Eva: Marion does?

Ronald: Oh, yes. Very nervous, insecure sort of person basically, you know.

Eva: Really?

Ronald: That surprises you, does it? Well, I've got a pretty thorough working knowledge of her now, you know. I mean, she's calmer than she was. When I first met her she was really one of the jumpiest girls you could ever hope to meet. Still, as I say, she's much calmer since she's been with me. If I've done nothing else for her, I've acted as a sort of sedative.

Eva: You don't think that a lot of her trouble may be—drink?

Ronald: Drink? No, I don't honestly think so. She's always liked a—I mean, the doctor did say she should lay off. But that was only because it was acting as a stimulant. She hasn't touched it lately.

Eva: She has this evening.

Ronald: Really?

Eva: Yes.

Ronald: Well, you do surprise me.

Eva: She's got quite a collection up there.

Ronald: Oh, has she? Has she now?

Eva: Didn't you know?

Ronald: Well, I don't often have much cause to go into her room these days. She likes her privacy, you see. And I respect that. Not that it's not a mutual arrangement, you understand. I mean, she doesn't particularly choose to come into my room either. So it works out rather conveniently. On the whole.

Eva: Do you ever see each other at all?

Ronald: Good Lord, it's not as if we aren't in the same house. We bang into each other quite frequently. It's not always as quiet as this, believe me. In the holidays we've got the boys here. They thump about. No end of a racket. Boys, of course. Mind you, they're no trouble—they're usually out, too, most of the time— with their friends.

Eva: Pity they're not with you for Christmas.

Ronald: Oh well, it's greatly over-estimated, this Christmas business. That reminds me, would you like a drink? Seeing as it's Christmas.

Eva: No, I don't think so.

Ronald: Oh, go on. Just one. With me, for Christmas.

Eva: Well—all right, a little one.

Ronald: Right. (*He rises*) Good. I'll brave the elements then and try and make it as far as the sitting-room . . .

The doorbell rings.

Eva: That's probably Geoff.

Ronald: (*opening the door*) I'll let him in, then. (*Stopping short*) Good Lord, is that dust on the hall table or frost? Won't be a minute.

Ronald goes out. Eva, alone, looks round the room rather sadly. She leaves the sandwich and plate on the table, puts

the other things back on the sideboard, returns to the table,
sits and starts to eat the sandwich. Geoffrey enters in his
overcoat.

Geoffrey: Blimey. Why aren't you sitting in the garden, it's warmer.
Eva: Hullo.
Geoffrey: Ready then?
Eva: I'm just going to have a drink with Ronnie.
Geoffrey: Oh. And how is *she?*
Eva: Drunk.
Geoffrey: God.

Pause. Eva munches.

Eva: How did you get on?
Geoffey: Well . . .
Eva: Did you ask him?
Geoffrey: Well . . .
Eva: You didn't.

Geoffrey does not reply.

You didn't damn well ask him.
Geoffrey: It's no good. I find it impossible to ask people for money.

Eva gives a short laugh.

I'm sorry.
Eva: He owes it you. You're not asking him a favour, you know. He
owes it you.
Geoffrey: I know.
Eva: Well then.
Geoffrey: It doesn't matter.
Eva: Oh, my . . . Oh well I'll have to get in touch with him then.
After Christmas. I don't mind doing it.

Geoffrey: You don't have to do that.
Eva: Well, somebody has to, darling. Don't they?

The door opens. A drinks trolley enters followed by Ronald.

Ronald: Here we come. The Trans-Siberian Express. Thank you so
much. We seem to be a bit depleted on the old alcohol stakes.
Odd, thought I'd stocked up only recently. Probably old Mrs.
Minns been knocking them off, eh? The woman must have some
vices. She hasn't got much else to recommend her. Now what are
we having. Eva?
Eva: Could I have just a bitter lemon.
Ronald: Good gracious, nothing stronger?
Eva: Not just now.
Ronald: Well, if that's what you want . . . Geoff, what about you?
Geoffrey: I think I'd like the same, actually.
Ronald: What? A bitter lemon?
Geoffrey: Just what I feel like.
Ronald: You won't last through Christmas at that rate. (*Inspecting
his trolley*) Well, that seems to be the only thing I haven't
brought.
Eva: Oh well, it doesn't matter. Something else.
Ronald: No, no. I'll get it, I'll get it. We've got some somewhere.

Ronald goes out, closing the door.

Eva: I mean, either you want me to help you or you don't.
Geoffrey: Yes.
Eva: I mean, if you don't just say so. I don't particularly enjoy work-
ing in that dark little office of yours. You're a terrible employer.
You come in late even when I drive you to work. You take four-
hour lunch breaks and then expect me to do all your damn typing
at five o'clock in the evening.
Geoffrey: That's the way I do business.

Eva: Not with me you don't.

Geoffrey: That's what you're paid for.

Eva: That's what I'm what?

Geoffrey: Look, if you don't like the job . . .

Eva: You asked me to help you. Now, if you didn't mean that, that's a different matter.

Geoffrey: Well yes, I did, but . . .

Eva: All right, then. That's settled. You asked me to help you. I am bloody well going to help you.

Geoffrey: O.K. O.K., thanks.

Eva: Not at all. (*A slight pause*) And you're not going to ask for that money?

Geoffrey: No.

Eva: Even though we're owed it?

Geoffrey: No.

Eva: And you won't let me ask?

Geoffrey: No.

Eva: All right. Then we'll have to think of something else.

Geoffrey: Exactly.

Eva: I'll phone Sidney Hopcroft after Christmas and talk to him.

Geoffrey: Sidney Hopcroft.

Eva: He's always asking if you're interested.

Geoffrey: If you think I'm going to get myself involved in his seedy little schemes . . .

Eva: Why not?

Geoffrey: Have you seen the buildings he's putting up? Half his tenants are asking to be re-housed and they haven't even moved in yet.

Eva: Darling, I hate to remind you but ever since the ceiling of the Harrison building caved in and nearly killed the manager, Sidney Hopcroft is about your only hope of surviving as an architect in this city.

Geoffrey: I can do without Sidney Hopcroft, thank you very much.

The door opens. Ronald enters with two bottles of bitter lemon.

Ronald: Here we are. Two very bitter lemons. (*He pours out two bitter lemons and a scotch*)

Eva: Thank you.

Ronald: I think I'm going to have something more than that, if you'll excuse me. Bit quieter than last Christmas, eh?

Geoffrey: What?

Ronald: Last Christmas. Remember that? Round at your place?

Geoffrey: Yes.

Eva: Yes.

Ronald: Good gracious me. You have to laugh now. Old Hopcroft. (*He laughs*) Always remember old Hopcroft. Doing very well. Did you know that? Doing frightfully well. Seems to have a flare for it. Wouldn't think so to look at him. Always found him a bit unprepossessing. Still—the chap to keep in with. The rate he's going.

Eva: Yes.

Geoffrey: (*picking up Ronald's book*) Is this good?

Ronald: Oh, yes. Yes, quite good. Very amusing. Bit—saucy, in parts. Mrs. Minns found it under one of the boys' mattresses. Nearly finished her there and then, poor old thing. Bitter lemon—

Eva: Thanks.

Ronald: Bitter lemon.

Geoffrey: Thank you.

Ronald: (*raising his glass of scotch*) Well, Happy Christmas. Good health. God bless.

Eva: Happy Christmas.

Geoffrey: Happy Christmas.

Ronald: (*after a pause*) Sorry to hear about your problems, Geoff.

Geoffrey: How do you mean?

Ronald: I meant, the Harrison thing. Hear it fell through . . . Oh,

I'm sorry, perhaps that's the wrong expression to use—bit unfortunate.

Geoffrey: That's all right.

Eva: It wasn't actually Geoff's fault.

Ronald: No, no, I'm sure—knowing Geoff. Unthinkable. I mean, that local paper's as biased as hell. I refused to read that particular article. So did all my friends.

Eva: (*after a pause*) Just because Geoffrey was doing something totally new for a change . . .

Geoffrey: How's the bank doing, then?

Ronald: Oh, well. We're not in the red, yet. No thanks to me, mind you.

A bell rings.

Ah.

Geoffrey: Is that the front door?

Ronald: No. It's the—er—bedroom bell, actually. We've never bothered to have them taken out. They always come in useful. Boys with measles and so on.

Eva: Shall I go up to her?

Ronald: No, no, I'll . . .

Eva: No, it's all right. I don't mind . . .

Ronald: Well, that's very good of you. Probably nothing important. Wants the page of her magazine turning over or something.

Eva: I hope not.

Ronald: What's the harm, I say. As long as it keeps her happy.

Eva: Yes.

Eva goes out, closing the door.

Ronald: I mean, who are we to argue with a woman, eh? You can never win. Hopeless. Mind you, I'm talking to the wrong chap, aren't I?

87

Geoffrey: What?

Ronald: I mean you seem to do better than most of us.

Geoffrey: Oh, yes. (*He sits in the armchair*)

Ronald: You seem to have got things pretty well organized on the home front. (*He laughs*)

Geoffrey: Well, it's just a matter of knowing . . .

Ronald: Ah yes, that's the point. I never really have. Not really. I mean, take my first wife. Distinguished-looking woman. Very charming. Seemed pretty happy on the whole. Then one day, she suddenly ups and offs and goes. Quite amazing. I mean, I had literally no idea she was going to. I mean, we had the flat over the bank at the time, so it wasn't as if I was even very far away and on this particular day, I came up for lunch and she'd laid on her usual splendid meal. I mean I had absolutely no complaints about that. I think my very words were something like, jolly nice that, see you this evening. And when we knocked off for tea, I came upstairs and she'd just taken off. Well, I hunted about for a bit in case she'd got knocked down or gone shopping and lost her memory or something and then she wrote, some time later, and said she'd had enough. So I was forced to call it a day. Some time later again, I took up tennis to forget her and married Marion. Of course, that's all forgotten now. All the same, sometimes in the evening I can't help sitting here and trying to work it all out. I mean, something happened. Something must have happened. I'm just not sure what. Anyway. Under the bridge, eh? All I'm saying really, is some people seem to have the hang of it and some of us just aren't so lucky.

Geoffrey: Hang of what?

Ronald: Well—this whole women business, really. I mean, this may sound ridiculous, but I've never to this day really known what most women think about anything. Completely closed book to me. I mean, God bless them, what would we do without them? But I've never understood them. I mean, damn it all, one minute you're having a perfectly good time and the next, you suddenly see them there like—some old sports jacket or something—literally beginning to come apart at the seams. Floods of tears, smashing your pots, banging the furniture about. God knows what. Both my wives, God bless them, they've given me a great deal of pleasure over the years but, by God, they've cost me a fortune in fixtures and fittings. All the same. Couldn't do without them, could we? I suppose. Want another one of those?

Geoffrey: No, thanks.

The door opens. Eva enters. Geoffrey rises and sits again.

Eva: (*coming in swiftly and closing the door*) Brrr.

Ronald: Ah.

Eva: Forgot to put my coat on. (*She puts her coat on*)

Ronald: Anything serious?

Eva: No. (*Kneeling by the stove to warm herself*) She says she wants to come down.

Ronald: Here? Is that wise?

Eva: She says she wants a Christmas drink with us since we're all here.

Ronald: Oh well. Sort of thing she does. Calls you all the way upstairs to tell you she's coming all the way downstairs. Your drink there.

Eva: Thanks.

Ronald: And how's that mad dog of yours? Still chewing up your guests?

Geoffrey: Er—no . . .

Eva: No, we had to—give him away.

Ronald: No, really?

Eva: Yes—he got a bit much. He was really getting so expensive to keep. And then these people we know who've got a farm—they said they'd have him.

Ronald: Oh, dear. I didn't know that. That's a shame.

Eva: Yes, it was an awful decision to make. We just felt—well . . .

Geoffrey: You did, you mean.

Eva: Darling, we couldn't afford to keep him.

Ronald: Well, old Dick Potter will be relieved, anyway. What did he have to have? Three stitches or something, wasn't it?

Eva: Something like that.

Ronald: Doesn't seem to have done him any harm, anyway. He should be half-way up some Swiss mountain by now. Hopefully, those two lads of ours are safely roped to him.

Eva: Oh, is that where they've gone?

Ronald: Yes. Something I always meant to take them on myself. Anyway, we'll have to do without old Dick to jolly us up this year, I suppose.

Geoffrey: That's a pity.

The door opens. Marion sweeps in. She wears a negligée. She stands dramatically and flings out her arms.

Marion: Geoff, darling, it's sweet of you and Eva to come round and see me.

Geoffrey: (*rising*) Oh, that's O.K.

Marion: No, you don't know how much it means to me. It really is terribly, terribly sweet of you.

Geoffrey: That's all right, we were . . .

Marion: And at Christmas, particularly. Bless you for remembering Christmas. (*She collapses into the armchair*)

Ronald: Look, Marion, you're going to freeze to death. For goodness' sake, put something on, woman.

Marion: I'm all right.

Ronald: Let me get you your coat. You've only just got out of bed.

Marion: Darling, I am quite all right. And I am not sitting in my kitchen in a coat. Nobody sits in a kitchen in a coat. Except tradesmen. It's unheard of. Now, offer me a drink.

Ronald: Look, dear, you know the doctor said very plainly . . .

Marion: (*snapping fiercely*) Oh, for the love of God, Ronnie, it's Christmas. Don't be such an utter misery. (*To the others*) He's

Scrooge, you know. He's Scrooge in person. Have you noticed, he's turned all the heating off.

Ronald, dignified, goes to the trolley and pours Marion a drink.

Oh, it's heavenly to be up. When you've lain in bed for any length of time, on your own, no-one to talk to, with just your thoughts, don't you find your whole world just begins to crowd in on you. Till it becomes almost unbearable. You just lie there thinking, oh God, it could've been so much better if only I'd had the sense to do so and so—you finish up lying there utterly filled with self-loathing.

Eva: I know the feeling.

Ronald: (*handing Marion a glass*) Here you are, dear.

Marion: Heavens! I can hardly see it. Is there anything in here? No it's all right. I'll just sit here and inhale it. (*Turning to Geoffrey and Eva*) How are you anyway?

Eva: Well, as I told you we're—pretty well . . .

Marion: I don't know what it is about Christmas but—I know it's supposed to be a festive thing and we're all supposed to be enjoying ourselves—I just find myself remembering all the dreadful things—the dreadful things I've said—the dreadful things I've done and all those awful hurtful things I didn't mean—oh God, I didn't mean them. Forgive me, I didn't mean them. (*She starts to cry*)

Ronald: Look, darling, do try and jolly up just for a bit, for heaven's sake.

Marion: (*savagely*) Jolly up? How the hell can—I—jolly—up?

Eva: Marion, dear . . .

Marion: Do you know what I saw in the hall just now? In the mirror. My face. My God, I saw my face. It was like seeing my face for the first time.

Ronald: Oh, come on. It's not a bad face, old sausage.

Marion: How could anything be so cruel? How could anything be so unutterably cruel?

Ronald: (*to Geoffrey*) Now, you see, this is a case in point. What am I supposed to do? I mean, something I've said has obviously upset her, but you tell me—you tell me.

Marion: (*pulling Geoffrey to her*) Geoff—Geoff—Geoff—did you know, Geoff, I used to be a very beautiful woman? I was a very, very beautiful woman. People used to stare at me in the street and say, "My God, what a beautiful, beautiful woman she is." People used to come from miles and miles just to take my picture . . .

Ronald: Marion.

Marion: I mean, who'd want my photograph now? Do you want my photograph now? No, of course you don't. Nobody wants my photograph now. Can anybody think of anyone who'd want a photograph of me now? Please, someone. Someone, please want my photograph.

Ronald: (*bellowing*) Marion! Nobody wants your damn picture, now shut up.

A silence. Geoffrey and Eva are stunned. Ronald removes his eyeshade and adjusts his scarf.

(*The first to recover*) Now then, what were we saying?

The doorbell rings.

Eva: (*after a pause*) Doorbell.

Ronald: Bit late for a doorbell, isn't it?

They sit. The doorbell rings again.

Eva: Shall I see who it is?

Ronald: Yes, do. Have a look through the little glass window. If you don't like the look of them, don't open the door.
Eva: Right.

Eva goes into the hall.

Ronald: Can't think who'd be ringing doorbells at this time of night.
Geoffrey: Carol singers?
Ronald: Not at this time. Anyway, we don't get many of them. Marion always asks them in. Insists on filling them up with hot soup and chocolate biscuits as if they were all starving. Had a great row with the chap next door. She made his children as sick as pigs.

Eva returns. As she does so the doorbell rings. She closes the door behind her.

Eva: I couldn't be sure but it looks suspiciously like the Hopcrofts. Do you want them in?
Ronald: Oh, good grief, hardly.
Geoffrey: Heaven forbid.
Ronald: If we sit quiet, they'll go away.
Eva: Well, there's the hall light.
Ronald: That doesn't mean anything. People always leave their hall lights on for burglars. I don't know why they bother. I mean, there must be very few households who actually choose to spend their evenings sitting in the hall with the rest of the house in the darkness.
Geoffrey: If I know the Hopcrofts, they won't give up easily. They'll come round the side.
Marion: Why don't you just go in the hall and shout "Go away" through the letter-box?
Ronald: Because he happens to have a very large deposit account with my bank.

The doorbell rings.

Eva: They can smell us.
Ronald: I think we'll compromise and turn off the lights in here. Just
    to be on the safe side. (*Going to the door*) Everybody sit down
    and sit tight. (*By the switch*) Ready? Here we go.

*The room plunges into darkness. Just two streams of light—
one from the door and one from the window.*

Now if we all keep absolutely quiet, there's no chance of them—
    ow! (*He cannons into Eva who gives a cry*) I'm terribly sorry. I do
    beg your pardon. Was that your . . . ?
Eva: That's all right.
Geoffrey: Ssh.
Ronald: I wish I knew where I was.
Geoffrey: Well, stand still. I think someone's coming round the side.
Eva: Ssh.

Marion starts to giggle.

Ronald: Marion. Quiet.
Marion: I'm sorry I've just seen the funny side . . .
Geoffrey: Ssh.

*Sidney and Jane appear at the back door. They wear party
hats, are decked with the odd streamer, have had more drinks
than they are used to and have a carrier bag full of goodies.
They both press their faces against the back door, straining
to see in.*

Marion: It's them.
Geoffrey: Ssh.

Pause.

Ronald: I say . . .
Eva: What?
Ronald: I've got a nasty feeling I didn't lock the back door.

Geoffrey and Eva hide in front of the table. Ronald steps up into a corner by the window. The back door opens slowly.

Sidney: Hallo?
Jane: (*unwilling to enter*) Sidney . . .
Sidney: Come on.
Jane: But there's nobody . . .
Sidney: The door was open, wasn't it? Of course there's somebody. They're probably upstairs.
Jane: But, Sidney, they might . . .
Sidney: Look, would you kindly not argue with me any more tonight, Jane. I haven't yet forgiven you for that business at the party. How did you manage to drop a whole plate of trifle?
Jane: I didn't clean it up, Sidney, I didn't clean it up.
Sidney: No. You just stood there with the mess at your feet. For all the world to see.
Jane: Well, what . . .
Sidney: I have told you before. If you drop something like that at a stand-up party, you move away and keep moving. Now come along.
Jane: I can't see.
Sidney: Then wait there and I'll find the light.

A pause. Sidney crosses the room. Geoffrey and Eva creep to the sideboard. The light goes on. Sidney and Jane are by the separate doors. The other four are in various absurd frozen postures obviously caught in the act of trying to find a hiding-place. Jane gives a short squeak of alarm. A long pause.

Marion: (*eventually*) Boo.
Sidney: Good gracious.
Ronald: (*as if seeing them for the first time*) Ah, hallo there. It's you.
Sidney: Well, you had us fooled. They had us fooled there, didn't they?
Jane: Yes, they had us fooled.
Sidney: Playing a game on us, weren't you?
All: Yes.
Eva: Yes, we were playing a game.
Sidney: Completely fooled. Walked straight into that. Well, Happy Christmas, all.
All: (*lamely, variously*) Happy Christmas.
Sidney: (*after a pause*) Well.
Jane: Well.

A *pause.*

Ronald: Would you like a drink? Now you're here.
Sidney: Oh, thank you.
Jane: Thank you very much.
Sidney: Since we're here.
Ronald: Well. What'll it be? (*He goes to the trolley*)
Sidney: Sherry, please.
Jane: Yes, a sherry.
Sidney: Yes. We'd better stick to sherry.
Ronald: Sherry . . . (*He starts to pour*)
Sidney: Sorry if we surprised you.
Marion: Quite all right.
Sidney: We knew you were here.
Ronald: How?
Sidney: We saw the car.
Jane: Saw your car.
Ronald: Oh. Yes.

A pause. Sidney blows a party "blower."

Eva: Been to a party?
Sidney: Yes.
Jane: Yes.
Geoffrey: You look as if you have.
Sidney: Yes. Up at Walter's place. Walter Harrison.
Ronald: Oh—old Harrison's.
Sidney: Oh of course, you'll know him, won't you?
Ronald: Oh, yes.
Geoffrey: Yes.
Sidney: (*to Geoffrey*) Oh, yes, of course. Asking you if you know old
   Harrison. I should think you do know old Harrison. He certainly
   remembers you. In fact he was saying this evening . . .
Ronald: Two sherries.
Sidney: Oh, thank you.
Jane: Thank you very much.
Sidney: Compliments of the season.
Jane: Of the season.
Ronald: Yes. Indeed.

A pause.

Sidney: What a house. Beautiful.
Marion: Oh, do you like it? Thank you.
Sidney: No. Old Harrison's. What a place.
Jane: Lovely.
Ronald: Didn't know you knew him.
Sidney: Well, I won't pretend. The reason we went was half pleasure
   and half—well, 'nuff said. Follow me? You scratch my back, I'll
   scratch yours.
Ronald: Ah.

A pause.

Jane: It's a nice kitchen . . .
Marion: At the Harrisons'?
Jane: No. Here.
Marion: Oh. Glad you approve.

A pause.

Jane: (*very, very quietly*) Sidney.
Sidney: Eh?
Jane: (*mouthing and gesticulating towards the carrier bag*) Their presents.
Sidney: What's that?
Jane: (*still mouthing and miming*) Shall we give them their presents now?
Sidney: Yes, yes, of course. That's why we've brought them.
Jane: We brought you a present.
Sidney: Just a little seasonal something.
Ronald: Oh.
Marion: Ah.
Eva: Thank you.
Jane: (*to Eva*) No, I'm afraid we didn't bring you and your husband anything. We didn't know you'd be here, you see.
Sidney: Sorry about that.
Eva: Oh, never mind.
Geoffrey: Not to worry.
Jane: We could give them the hm-mm. You know that we got given this evening.
Sidney: The what?
Jane: You know, the hm-mm. That we got in the thing.
Sidney: What, that? They don't want that.
Jane: No, I meant for hm-mm, you know. Hm-mm.
Sidney: Well, if you want to. Now, come on. Give Ron and Marion their presents. They're dying to open them.
Ronald: Rather.

Marion: Thrilling.

Jane: (*delving into her carrier and consulting the labels on various parcels*) Now this is for Ron. (*Reading*) To Ron with love from Sidney and Jane.

Sidney: (*handing Ronald the present*) That's for you.

Ronald: Thank you. (*He unwraps it*)

Jane: Now then, what's this?

Sidney: Is that Marion's?

Jane: No, that's from you and me to Auntie Gloria. (*Rummaging again*) Here we are. To Marion with love from Sidney and Jane.

Sidney: This is for you. (*He gives Marion her present*)

Marion: Oh, super . . . (*To Ronald*) What've you got, darling?

Ronald: (*gazing at his present mystified*) Oh, yes. This is very useful. Thank you very much.

Marion: What on earth is it?

Ronald: Well, it's—er—(*taking a stab at it*)—looks like a very nice set of pipe cleaners.

Jane: Oh, no.

Sidney: No, those aren't pipe cleaners.

Ronald: Oh, aren't they?

Sidney: Good gracious, no.

Ronald: Oh, no. Silly of me. Just looked terribly like them for a minute. From a certain angle.

Sidney: You should know those. It's a set of screwdrivers.

Jane: Set of screwdrivers.

Sidney: Electrical screwdrivers.

Jane: You should know those, shouldn't you?

Sidney and Jane laugh. Marion opens her present.

Marion (*with a joyous cry*) Oh, look! It's a lovely bottle of gin. Isn't that kind?

Ronald: Oh, my God.

Sidney: Bit of Christmas spirit.

Marion: Lovely. I'll think of you when I'm drinking it.
Jane: (*still rummaging*) To the boys with love from Sidney and Jane. (*She produces two rather ghastly woolly toys—obviously unsuitable*)
Sidney: That's just a little something.
Jane: For their stockings in the morning.
Marion: Oh, how nice.
Ronald: They'll love these . . .
Sidney: That the lot?
Jane: No, I'm just trying to find the hm-mm.
Sidney: Well, it'll be at the bottom somewhere, I should think.
Jane: I've got it. It's nothing very much. We just got it this evening out of a cracker actually. We were going to keep it for our budgie but we thought your George might like it. For his collar. (*She holds up a little bell on a ribbon*)
Eva: Oh.
Sidney: So you'll know where he is.
Jane: As if you couldn't guess.

Sidney barks genially and hands them the bell.

Sidney: Woof woof!
Eva: Thank you.
Sidney: (*to Geoffrey*) Woof woof. (*No response*) Woof woof.
Geoffrey: (*flatly*) Thanks a lot.
Sidney: That's your lot. No more.
Ronald: I'm terribly sorry. I'm afraid we haven't got you anything at all. Not really much of ones for present buying.
Sidney: Oh, we didn't expect it.
Jane: No, no.

A pause. Sidney puts on a nose mask. Jane laughs. The others look horrified. Marion pours herself a gin.

Sidney: Well—(*he pauses*)—you know who ought to be here now?

Jane: Who?

Sidney: Dick Potter. He'd start it off.

Jane: With a bit of help from Lottie.

Sidney: True. True.

Ronald: Yes, well, for some odd reason we're all feeling a bit low this evening. Don't know why. But we were just all saying how we felt a bit down.

Jane: Oh . . .

Sidney: Oh dear oh dear.

Ronald: Just one of those evenings, you know. The point is you'll have to excuse us if we're not our usual cheery selves.

Marion: I'm perfectly cheery. I don't know about anybody else.

Ronald: That is apart from my wife who is perfectly cheery.

Sidney: Oh, that's quite understood.

Jane: I have those sometimes, don't I?

Sidney: You certainly do. You can say that again. Well, that's a shame.

Ronald: Yes.

Eva: (*after a slight pause*) My husband was saying to me just now, Sidney, that he feels terribly guilty that you keep on asking him to do jobs for you and he just hasn't been able to manage them.

Sidney: Yes. Well, he's a busy man.

Eva: Sometimes. But he really is dying to do something for you before long.

Geoffrey: Eh?

Eva: He's really longing to.

Sidney: Oh, well in that case, we'll see.

Eva: If you could keep him in mind.

Sidney: Yes, I'll certainly keep him in mind. Really rather depends.

Geoffrey: Yes, it does rather.

Eva: He'd love to.

Sidney: (*after a pause*) Well now, what shall we do? Anyone got any ideas? We can't all sit round like this, can we? Not on Christmas Eve.

Jane: No, not on Christmas Eve.

Sidney: Spot of carpentry, spot of plumbing, eh? I know what about a spot of electrical work. (*At the radio*) Well, we can have a bit of music to start off with, anyway. (*To Ronald*) This work all right, does it?

Ronald: Yes, yes, but I wouldn't . . .

Sidney: Get the party going, bit of music . . . (*He switches on the radio and begins to dance a little*)

Jane: Bit of music'll get it going.

Sidney: Hey . . .

Jane: What?

Sidney: You know what we ought to do now?

Jane: What?

Sidney: We ought to move all the chairs back and clear the floor and . . .

The radio warms up and the room is filled with the sound of an interminable Scottish reel which plays continually. Like most Scottish reels, without a break. This effectively drowns the rest of Sidney and Jane's discussion. He continues to describe with graphic gestures his idea to Jane. Jane claps her hands with excitement. They move the table, stove and chairs out of the way. Sidney then wheels the trolley away past Marion's armchair. She grabs a bottle as it goes by.

Ronald: (*yelling above the noise*) What the hell's going on?

Sidney: (*yelling back*) You'll see. Just a minute. (*He turns the radio down a little*) Now then. We can't have this. We can't have all these glum faces, not at Christmas time.

Jane: (*scurrying about collecting a bowl of fruit, a spoon, a tea-cosy, colander and tea towel from the dresser and draining-board*) Not at Christmas time. (*She opens the gin bottle and puts a glass near it on the trolley*)

Sidney: So we're going to get you all jumping about. Get you cheerful.

Ronald: No, well I don't think we really . . .

Sidney: No arguments, please.

Ronald: Yes, but all the same . . .

Sidney: Come on then, Eva, up you get.

Eva: (*uncertainly*) Well . . .

Sidney: Come on. Don't you let me down.

Eva: No . . . (*She rises*)

Geoffrey: I'm afraid we both have to . . .

Eva: No, we don't. We'll play.

Geoffrey: What do you mean, we'll . . .

Eva: If he wants to play, we'll play, darling.

Jane begins to roll up the carpet.

Sidney: That's grand. That's marvellous. That's two—come on—any more?

Marion: What are we all doing? Is she going to be terribly sweet and wash our floor?

Jane: No, we're playing a game.

Sidney: A game.

Marion: Oh, what fun . . .

Ronald: Marion, I really don't think we should . . .

Marion: Oh, don't be such a misery, Ronnie. Come on.

Ronald: Oh . . .

Sidney: That's telling him, that's telling him. Now then listen very carefully, everyone. This is a version of musical chairs called Musical Dancing.

Jane: Musical Forfeits.

Sidney: Musical Dancing. It's called Musical Dancing.

Jane: Oh, I thought it was called Musical Forfeits.

Sidney: Musical Dancing. It's very simple. All you do—you start dancing round the room and when I stop the music you all have to freeze in the position you were last in . . .

Geoffrey sits on the high stool.

Don't let him sit down. (*To Geoffrey*) Come on, get up.

Eva: (*sharply*) Get up.

Geoffrey gets up.

Sidney: Only to make it more difficult, the last person caught moving each time gets a forfeit. At the end, the person with the least forfeits gets the prize. (*To Jane*) What's the prize going to be?

Jane: (*producing it from the carrier*) A chocolate Father Christmas.

Sidney: A chocolate Father Christmas, right. Everything ready your end?

Jane: I think so.

Sidney: Got the list?

Jane: (*waving a scrap of paper*) Yes.

Sidney: Right. You take charge of the forfeits. I'll do the music. Ready, everybody? Right. Off we go.

Sidney turns up the music loud. The four stand looking faintly uneasy. Jane and Sidney dance about to demonstrate.

Well, come on then. Come on. I don't call that dancing. Everybody dance. Come on, dance about. Keep dancing till the music stops.

Marion starts to dance, in what she imagines to be a classical ballet style. She is extremely shaky.

That's it. She's doing it. That's it. Look at her. Everybody do what she's doing. Lovely.

The others begin sheepishly and reluctantly to hop about.

And—stop! (*He cuts off the music*) Right. Who was the last?
Jane: Ron.
Sidney: Right. It's Ron. Ron has a forfeit. What's the first one?
Jane: (*consulting her list*) Apple under the chin.
Sidney: Apple under his chin, right. Put an apple under his chin.
Ronald: Eh? What are you doing?

Jane puts the apple under his chin.

Jane: Here. Hold it. Go on, hold it.
Ronald: Oh, don't be so ridiculous, I can't possibly . . .
Marion: Oh, for heaven's sake, darling, do join in. We're all waiting for you. Don't be tedious.
Ronald: (*talking with difficulty*) This is absolutely absurd, I mean how am I to be . . .
Sidney: (*over this*) And off we go again. (*He turns up the music*)

They resume dancing. Marion is the only one who moves around: the others jig about on one spot. Sidney shouts encouragement.

And—stop! (*He stops the music*)
Jane: Eva!
Sidney: Right, Eva. What's Eva got?
Jane: (*consulting list*) Orange between the knees.
Sidney: Orange between the knees, right. If you drop it you get another forfeit automatically.

Jane gives Eva her orange.

And off we go again.

Music. From now on the forfeits come quick and fast. Jane reading them out, Sidney repeating them. Ronald gets the next (spoon in mouth). The music continues. Geoffrey gets the next (tea-cosy on head). They dance on. Marion gets the next (ironically, swallowing a gin in one). Ronald opens his mouth to protest at this last forfeit of Marion's. In doing so he drops his spoon.

(*Gleefully*) Another one for Ron!
Jane: Another one for Ron . . .
Ronald: What?
Jane: Pear on spoon in mouth . . .
Sidney: Pear on spoon in mouth . . . (*He gets up on the table and conducts*)
Ronald: Now listen I . . .

Jane rams the spoon handle back in Ronald's mouth. She balances a pear on the other end.

Sidney: And off we go . . . !

The permutations to this game are endless and Sidney's list covers them all. Under his increasingly strident commands, the dancers whirl faster and faster while accumulating bizarre appendages. Jane, the acolyte, darts in and out of the dancers with a dedicated frenzy. Geoffrey throws his tea-cosy to the floor. Jane picks it up and wraps a tea towel round his leg. She then pours another gin for Marion. Sidney, at the finish, has abandoned the idea of stopping the music. He screams at the dancers in mounting exhortation bordering on the hysterical.

That's it. Dance. Come on. Dance. Dance. Come on. Dance. Dance. Dance. Keep dancing. Dance . . .

It is on this scene that—

the curtain falls